MOVIE THERAPY, MOVING THERAPY!

by
Fuat Ulus, MD

The Healing Power of Film Clips in the Therapeutic Settings

Printed in Victoria, Canada

National Library of Canada Cataloguing in Publication Data

Ulus, Fuat
      Movie therapy, moving therapy / Fuat Ulus.

Includes bibliographical references.
ISBN 1-55395-705-9

      I. Title.

RC489.M654U48 2003   616.89'165   C2003-900468-6

This book was published *on-demand* in cooperation with Trafford Publishing.
On-demand publishing is a unique process and service of making a book available for retail sale to the public taking advantage of on-demand manufacturing and Internet marketing. **On-demand publishing** includes promotions, retail sales, manufacturing, order fulfilment, accounting and collecting royalties on behalf of the author.

Suite 6E, 2333 Government St., Victoria, B.C. V8T 4P4, CANADA
Phone   250-383-6864   Toll-free 1-888-232-4444 (Canada & US)
Fax   250-383-6804   E-mail   sales@trafford.com
Web site www.trafford.com   TRAFFORD PUBLISHING IS A DIVISION OF TRAFFORD HOLDINGS LTD.
Trafford Catalogue #03-0068   www.trafford.com/robots/03-0068.html

10   9   8   7   6   5   4   3   2

TABLE OF CONTENTS

ACKNOWLEDGMENTS

PREFACE

INTRODUCTION

HOW DO MOVIES AFFECT US?

OUR OWN INNER MOVIE CLIPS WE SUPPRESS, PROMOTE OR ABUSE!
FIGURE 1 SIX MODES OF OUR INTRAPSYCHIC COMPARTMENTS
FIGURE 2 EMOTICONS OF OUR SIX MODES

WHAT DOES LOVE & HATE HAVE TO DO WITH IT?

A MAN FOR ALL SEASONS: ONE ACTOR PLAYS ALL SIX MODES!

WHICH PATIENTS ARE REFERRED TO MOVIE GROUP THERAPY?

WHAT MAY BE THE THEMES FOR MOVIE GROUP THERAPY?

HOW DOES MOVIE GROUP THERAPY WORK?
FIGURE 3 MOVIE GROUP THERAPY DYNAMICS

WHO CAN BE A MOVIE GROUP THERAPIST?

HOW ABOUT PAYMENTS AND BILLINGS?

STAIRWAYS BEHAVIORAL HEALTH OUTPATIENT CLINIC
GROUP MOVIE THERAPY EXPERIENCE

SAMPLES FROM MOVIE CLIPS GALLERY:

MOVIE THERAPY WITHIN THE MOVIE THERAPY!
HANNAH AND HER SISTERS (1986)

PSYCHODRAMA IN A BARN?
AGNES OF GOD (1985)

THE RUNAWAY BUNNY!
WIT (2001)

SLAPPING EACH OTHER AND..THEN, *WHAT*?
RULES OF THE MARRIAGE (1984)

IS WHAT IS LOGICAL RIGHT, WRONG OR NEITHER?
JUDGMENT AT NUREMBERG (1961)

...BUT I DID TRY, DIDN'T I, GOD DAMN IT! ...LEAST, I DID THAT!
ONE FLEW OVER THE CUCKOO'S NEST (1975)

GO AHEAD...MAKE MY DAY!
SUDDEN IMPACT (1983)

ONE WORD...MANY MESSAGES!
THE BRIDGE ON THE RIVER KWAI (1957)

I WANT MY COFFEE IN A CUP!
KISS TOMORROW GOODBYE (1950)

WHO FORGIVES GOD FOR THE HOLOCAUST?
THE QUARREL (1991

WHEN YOU HAVE TO SHOOT, SHOOT! DON'T TALK!
THE GOOD, THE BAD AND THE UGLY (1966)

I LOVE MY PATIENT...
LOVESICK (1983)

I HATE MY PATIENT...
ANALYSE THIS (1999)

INTENSE COMMUNICATION WITH NO WORDS!
YOL (1981)

DOCTOR-PATIENT ROLE REVERSAL IN THE OFFICE...
DUET FOR ONE (1986)

"OLD BLOOD'N'GUTS" BEING ANXIETY THERAPIST?
PATTON (1970)

SPEAK SLOWLY AND CARRY A BIG STICK!
MILLER'S CROSSING (1990)

WE DON'T NEED TO TRUST EACH OTHER...WE ARE DOING BUSINESS!
SCAM (1993)

THE SHORTEST SUM IN THE LONGEST DAY!
THE LONGEST DAY (1962)

ASSERTIVE CHAT IN…THE MILITARY?
BATTLE OF THE BULGE (1965)

BOOZING UP, DOC?
THE HOSPITAL (1971)

JUDD HIRSCH, MY MOST FAVORITE MOVIE SHRINK!
ORDINARY PEOPLE (1980)

COMPETENT TO MAKE …A WRONG DECISION?
WHOSE LIFE IS IT ANYWAY (1981)

MARRIAGE BY …THE LOGIC?
SCENES FROM THE MALL (1991)

SAM PECKINPAH'S HUMOR THERAPY!?
WILD BUNCH (1969)

APPENDIX A-PSYCHIATRIST PORTRAYALS IN THE US PRODUCED
MOVIES BETWEEN 1906 AND 2002

APPENDIX B-PSYCHIATRIST PORTRAYALS IN THE INTERNATIONAL
MOVIES PRODUCED BETWEEN 1906 AND 1990

APPENDIX C-PSYCHIATRIST PORTRAYALS IN SOME
INTERNATIONAL MOVIES PRODUCED BETWEEN
1990 AND 2002

APPENDIX D-HIGHLIGHTS FROM THE WORKSHOP, "THE GOOD, THE BAD
AND THE UGLY", AMERICAN PSYCHIATRIC ASSOCIATION
INSTITUTE OF PSYCHIATRIC SERVICES, ORLANDO, FL
OCTOBER 10-14,2001

APPENDIX E-THE LIST OF THE AUTHOR'S PRESENTATIONS RELATED TO
THE COMMERCIAL MOVIES AND THEIR USE IN THE
EDUCATION & THERAPY

APPENDIX F-THE MOVIES, EDUCATION, TREATMENT AND HEALING
NETWORK; THE E-MAIL FORUM CONSISTED OF THE
PSYCHIATRISTS, PSYCHOLOGISTS, SOCIAL WORKERS,
INSTRUCTORS AND EDUCATORS WHO USE COMMERCIAL
MOVIES & MOVIE CLIPS IN THEIR EDUCATIONAL
AND TREATMENT SETTING

REFERENCES & SUGGESTED READINGS, BOOKS, ARTICLES, INTERVIEWS, WORKSHOPS, WEBSITES AND OTHER WORKS RELEVANT TO FILM/CINEMA/REEL/MOVIE THERAPY

ABOUT THE AUTHOR

ACKNOWLEDGEMENTS

Thank you Fusun
for bearing with the husband who kept making movie star impressions and acting scenes from the movie clips for more than twenty-seven years of marriage!

Thank you Eda
for refining the grammar, syntax and diction qualities of the whole manuscript!

Thank you also for co-chairing some of the American Psychiatric Association workshop presentations during the annual meetings!

Thank you Ece
for coordinating the Group Movie Therapy conference arranged by the University of Pittsburgh, Pittsburgh, Pennsylvania!

Thank you Dr. Leslie Rabkin
for your generosity in allowing the writer to use countless references extracted from your book, *"THE CELLULOID COUCH, An Annotated International Filmography of the Mental Health Professional in the Movies and Television, from the Beginning to 1990, Scarecrow Press, Inc., 1998"* The said information has not only been instrumental in promoting the quality of workshop mentioned in the different chapter of this book but has also been inspirational for the publication of this Group Movie Therapy work. You were kind enough to continue providing further information relevant to the movies produced after 1990. The author listed them and gave all the credits to you in those appropriate chapters. The only regret for the writer was his not being able to know you personally although the rare but long telephone chats these two movie buffs had have always been very festive occasions for both parties.

Thank you the LISTSERV members
THE MOVIES, EDUCATION, TREATMENT AND HEALING NETWORK
for your time and energy invested in the movie therapy and assisting the author to form and promote many ideas documented in this work! Your websites, interviews, presentations, seminars, books and articles relevant to this matter have been great help to the author.

Thank you TRAFFORD
for giving the author this chance to publish his very first book at the age of sixty!

PREFACE

The author walked with Gary Cooper, laughed with Richard Widmark, cried with Bette Davis, talked to Rita Hayworth, ran away from James Cagney, was scared to death of Robert Mitchum, loved Audrey Hepburn, rode with John Wayne, watched Marilyn Monroe, adored Laureen Bacall, danced with Astaire & Rogers, sang with Frankie Laine...

Yes, he did all these... while watching movies, of course!

You guessed right. He is a movie buff!

There were no computer tricks, color fascinations, sensaround technology and/or special effects in the movies he watched while he was growing up. Everything has been based on the powerful acting quality of the given actor or actress.

Those artists were bigger than life on the silver screen. Even the ugliest criminals and psychopaths were still able to send chills to the audience's spines without using those words that classify the picture "R" rated in contemporary times! Their looking at their victims was enough "to kill!"

The person who has been responsible of his initiation to the movie addiction was his mother. Although, his dad and brother too were fond of the movies, her influence has been exemplary. His wife and daughters continued the tradition later on, and movies became a part of the daily life for the Ulus family.

There was also a movie theater culture in the good old days. Those of you who have seen *The Cinema Paradiso* may have an idea about it. People used to go to the movies for socio-familial gatherings as well. People also used to get together, mutually making impressions of the actors and actresses after the movie.

The writer drove his spouse and daughters crazy with the said tradition throughout the years reflective of the said movie culture. Well, aforementioned actors and actresses were "impressionable" in those years. Can you make an impression of Ethan Hawke, Johnny Depp, Ben Affleck, Gwyneth Paltrow, Sharon Stone or Kate Blanchett? These young generation stars are as powerful as their silver screen predecessors and yet, the writer can not make any impressions of them. He either is losing his touch or out of his time!

Do you disagree? Well, go ahead bring them over if you do and I will bring Clark Gable, Gary Grant, James Stewart, Joan Crawford, Maureen O' Hara and Gloria Grahame with me!

Of course, the writer was not Rich Little or Frank Gorshin but enacted the scene when it corresponded to the real life matter. Do you remember Brian Benben's Martin Tupper character in 1990-96 FOX/HBO TV series, *Dream On*? Well, he was the same! He was automatically recalled a corresponding movie scene once he was confronted by the problem in the real life. Finally, the author's obsession to do that constantly generated an idea in his daughters' minds one day. They suggested consolidating his movie addiction into his trade, using it in education along with treatment and... leaving household alone!

Well, it was the beginning of his interest in using movie clips in the realm of group therapy!

This is what the whole book is about!

INTRODUCTION

The author who has a lifetime passion for movies shares the educational and therapeutic values of the film clips regarding their impact on our pursuit of happiness throughout our lives. The commercial movies and their respective clips ARE progressively becoming quite effective tools for educators and therapists alike since the early eighties. Although the literature and research have not yet been documenting their values as relevant and validated as some other fields of behavioral health, their importance has not yet been easily dismissed either.

Unlike many educators and therapists who use the whole movie for any given purpose, theme and/or setting, the author shows the clips and vignettes corresponding to simply, concretely and specifically defined problems, solutions for which the groups are formed. This book, therefore, is not about the psychoanalysis of films, neither is the reader expected to view films in its entirety unless a specific reason necessitates doing so. Our attention, therefore, centralizes around the scenes of commercial motion pictures.

The workshop, "The Good, The Bad and The Ugly, Hollywood's Portrayal of the Psychiatrists", chaired by the author and Eda Ulus, BS, his daughter during the American Psychiatric Association's Institute of Psychiatric Services annual meeting held in Orlando, FL during October 2001 (see the appropriate chapter) provides the nuclear material for this book. That is why the majority of those movie titles are reflective of the films produced in the US.

The ingenious statement, reflective of Freud's The Ego and The Id, "***It is possible for thought processes to become conscious through a reversion to visual residues in many people, this seems to be a favorite method... thinking in pictures... approximates more closely to unconscious processes than does thinking in words, and it is unquestionably older than the latter both ontogenetically and philogenetically,*** presented in Dr. Rabkin's Book (see Acknowledgement Chapter) before the *Contents* reminds us that Freud inadvertently conceptualizes the movie therapy long before Karl Menninger's Bibliotherapy, thought by most to be the prototype of imagery and its use in counseling during the forties and fifties!

The list of international productions depicting psychiatrists is given in different chapters proportionate to Dr. Rabkin's monumental work in his book and gracious information he further provided to the author during the publication of this work.

HOW DO MOVIES EFFECT US?

There are three main levels of communication theorized by Transactional Analysis, a simple, applicable and practical version of classical psychoanalysis (Figure I).

The movies may address the PARENTAL level where our convictions, beliefs, and traditions are located. The complimentary films for this parameter would be related to mores, education, history, religion, ethics, rights vs. wrongs, and SHOULDs-HAVE TOs-MUSTs. Novelty, creativity and innovations either may be rebuffed or accepted, depending upon polarizations of our negative and positive parental selves.

Our ADULT level would be watching for a qualified direction, acting, production, screen playing, photography, editing and all other promotions. Anything related to reason, logic, problem solving, workable vs. unworkable platforms, would be thought provoking pearls for the watcher.

The films with musical scores, songs, soundtracks, special effects, fantasies, good vs. bad themes, comedies & dramas would tickle our feelings and emotions placed on our CHILD level of functioning on the conscious level. The imageries and subliminal messages may also intentionally as well as inadvertently affect our unconscious, the compartment of our mind about which we are not consciously aware.

Of course, all movies have some mixture of these three levels.

We also choose to watch a given motion picture for a reason. Our CHILD may just want to have "a ha-ha, hi-hi" time regardless of the quality of the film. The ADULT may intend to watch a good thought provoking one. Finally, the PARENT may like to reinvigorate some mores through the story. That explains why two people whose characteristics are quite alike may still have different ideas about the same movie they watch together. One may admire the acting (ADULT), while the other one is bored (CHILD)! The movie may fascinate one by the historical facts (PARENT), while the other one may find the directing very poor (ADULT)! One may be thrilled by the action in the movie (CHILD), while the other one is disgusted by "R rated words" frequently used by the heroes/heroines (PARENT)!

We also have various tastes regarding those different expectations in any given stage in time. The author, for example, does not necessarily like to watch a psychological thriller after the long day during which he provides care for the emotionally afflicted adults. He prefers to watch The Three Stooges! The weekend, however, is different.

The movies provide and promote mediums by which we communicate with the others and ourselves. Even the film rebuffed by the majority of people may still be appealing to a few. That is the reason the author disagrees with the movie critics. Actually, their job is to present ALL positives and negatives for the given film. What they usually do, however, is either finding the film worthless or over sensationalizing it; quite an interesting extreme polarization corresponding to those levels of a given PARENT, ADULT and CHILD orientations!

OUR OWN INNER MOVIE CLIPS THAT WE SUPPRESS, PROMOTE OR ABUSE

Kindly review Figures 1 and 2...

What do you see there?

Six different modes that we need to understand if we are going to make some sense out of the mechanisms by which movie clips affect us...

We all are born with instincts, emotions and feelings. They cannot be adopted from someone or something. They are with us throughout our lives for the good, the bad and the ugly occasions! They are polarized to "Good Child" and "Bad Kid"; the twins constantly struggling to practice what makes them happy on our Child Level of Functioning. Our Good Child wants everybody be happy while our Bad Kid seeks selfish pleasure satisfactions.

We seek immediate gratifications while we grow up. We want to do what we want to do to serve our instincts and emotions to feel good! Well, some entity tames this drive down. Can you guess what it is?

Yes, you guessed right! It is initially our literal parents and parent substitutes and later on, the school, the faith community, the law and etc.

Depending on the quantity and quality of the parent and child relationship, it is assumed us to adopt the regulation, accept our limitations and act like our parents. Here, we start to formalize our own Parental level of functioning. We create "a mini-parent" in us, what we may later call "a conscience." This becomes a thermostat of properly experiencing as well as expressing our instincts and emotions.

Human nature, however, has potential for vacillation between the extremes! Think of Felix, the punctual, clean, meticulous, responsible, over-organized and model citizen of the Odd Couple Duo... He represents one unhealthy extreme of SUBMISSION to this parental regulation at the expense of his own autonomy, creativity, innovation and productivity. His buddy Oscar, on the other hand, ends up with being a practitioner of the opposite unhealthy extreme of REVOLUTION! He is untidy, disorderly, hedonistic, dirty and irresponsible...with not much to be useful for society! The balance, therefore, between our "twins" on the Child level of functioning is important, as they are not expected to overtake each other's domain at anybody's expense.

Speaking of the said balance, the Parental level of functioning too has its "twins!" Take a minute or two and evaluate what kind of parent we are or would be if we are not in that position... Are we critical? Accepting? Nurturing? Controlling? Teaching? Prohibiting? Forgiving & Forgetting? Punishing?

The polarization we mentioned to happen where our instincts and emotions are transacted has the potential to generate and maintain itself on the Parental Level as well. Both extremes are unhealthy. A cruel parental authority is as unhealthy as Polly Anna type of ineffective parental figure! The balance, therefore, is very important to generate healthy "monitoring" designed for the given child who is in a process of growing up.

Well, we also notice our Adult level of functioning, do we not?

What is it?

Let us answer another question before we figure out the answer: What makes the human being superior to other creatures living on this earth?

Strength? Rhino-and relatively even an ant- are stronger than us! Speed? Look at the cheetah! Beauty? The butterfly is the best! Working capacity? Do not forget the bees! Ability to foresee the future? All animals do that better during the few moments prior to the natural disaster!

Well, what then?

Our reasoning capacity! (Watch the clip from Inherit the Wind about which information has already been given in another chapter regarding Spencer Tracy)

Yes, our reasoning, rational thinking, learning from previous experiences, using the algorithmic problem resolution options, assertiveness-defending what we think without putting down others-problem solving capacities, avoiding our convictions and emotions interfering with the decision making processes and in one word THINKING separates us from the animal kingdom.

Well, this leads to another question: What is thinking?

For the sake of mnemonics, it consists of six Rs!

Reception: We receive information from our environment through our five senses.

Registration: We review the qualities of the information.

Relocation: We place the information in the designated areas of our brain.

Review: We evaluate the already stored information if and when we receive other material, now leading and necessitating us to make a decision.

Reasoning: Mini algorhytmic scale on which the options are compared with each other regarding their outcomes, and

Response: We act-and not react-based on our problem solving capacity staged on the said previous transactions.

Our Adult functional level, therefore, is developed and maintained for this purpose!

The Adult level of functioning is not immune to polarization either. In one direction, there is a reflection of Mr. Spock, Sergeant Friday, Clint Eastwood and other characterizations...The Negative Adult generates and maintains work based entirely upon the reasoning! There are no emotions, instincts, convictions, beliefs or traditions! "That's the Way It is" theme dominates... At the other extreme, there stands the Positive Adult whose actions, like the counterpart, reflect the reasoning quality. However, the Positive Adult also displays compassion for self AS WELL AS others. S/he listens, is assertive-respects what others feel, think and believe while s/he asserts him/herself without putting down the opposition, reviews the options and alternatives, prioritizes the necessities and tries to come up with the best solution to serve everybody's best interest.

The Adult level of functioning has differences in comparison to the two other levels as follows:

By the late teens or early twenties both Parent and Child levels of functioning crystallize into the characteristics observed during most of our lives! There is always room for improvement, on the other hand, for the Adult level of functioning. Based upon our other qualities and capacities, a human being with average intelligence can always make his/her thinking better within the perspective of problem solving throughout one's life.

The writer has two analogies in making this point:

Think of the crocodile... Its upper jaw is Parental while the lower one represents the Child level of functioning. The crocodile snaps each time when it reacts to nature around it, e.g. fear, danger, nourishment, etc. This is the same way that we do! We REACT either with our convictions & beliefs (Upper Jaw) or instincts & feelings (Lower Jaw) to our environment. Once formed, there is almost no change the way these jaws react with the exception of time's effect on both of them. The Adult level of functioning represents the action we have between those powerful jaws. That is why we have difficulty in responding through ACTING rather than REACTING; as they say it takes 400 pounds of pressure to hold the crocodile's jaws apart! We need, therefore, a corresponding effort to keep away the Parent & Child interferences, when we make a decision based on reason. Keep in mind that our effort to keep them apart; processing through reason, is more easier than expecting the jaws' change; a process may only be achieved through time effecting our emotions, convictions and etc!

Form a cup using your hands... Bring your right hand fingers tips of which to touch the tips of left hand fingers. Slide them until the tips of eight fingers would not move further, creating the seesaw cup, both palms up. Your right index finger is between your left index finger and your left middle finger, your left middle finger is between your right index finger and right middle finger, and so on and so forth. The tips of your thumbs touch each other...Your right hand correspondences with Parental while your left hand represents Child level of functioning, they can not change proportionate to the crocodile's jaws! What may change is the quantity and quality of thinking we put in our "cup." This is Adult level of functioning and again, there is always room for quick improvement here than that of Parental and Child level functions.

The adult level of functioning has secondary effects in addition to its primary qualities:

It delegates the proper mode for the given occasion!

Are we to stage a fight with a shady character immediately threatening our family?

Send out the Bad Kid!

May we have decent fun during the festivity?

Wake up the Good Child!

Do we need our composure to help others during/after the disaster?

Assign the Negative Adult!

Is someone's behavior out of control?

Post the Negative Parent!

Are we intending to forgive and forget?

Let the Positive Parent help!

All these modes are useful for different occasions if the delegated level of functioning would always be within moderation.

Of interest, one may think that those three levels of TA functioning may be corresponding to Freud's Id (Child) / Ego (Adult) / Superego (Parent) hypothesis.

Transactional Analysis, after all, is a variant of classical psychoanalysis. What intrigues me is all of us using the word "Ego" to characterize "the Id" in our daily lives, e.g., "Someone's ego trip!" "Oh, this is a matter of his/her ego" and etc. I have distanced myself from classical psychoanalysis for decades, but this may be an interesting debate subject regarding the further clarification of the matter. We misuse Ego to represent our pride (Parent) and/or selfishness (Child) while its counterpart Adult level of functioning in TA disavows both!

Figure 1

𝕹egative Parent   *Positive Parent*

Level of Convictions, beliefs and traditions

WRONG vs. RIGHT

CRITICAL, CONTROLLING, PATRONIZING, PUNISHING, NARROW-MINDED, "SHOULD-HAVE TO-MUST" ORIENTATIONS	TEACHING, GUIDING, LIMIT-SETTING, NOURISHING, ACCEPTING, FORGIVING & FORGETTING

ΠEGAΞIVE AƉULΞ   POSITIVE ADULT

Level of reason, logic and factuality

UNWORKABLE vs. WORKABLE

BY-THE-BOOK, FACT-ORIENTED, "THAT'S THE WAY IT IS", "SHAPE UP OR SHIP OUT" ORIENTATION	ASSERTIVE, PROBLEM-SOLVING, COMPASSIONATE FOR SELF AND OTHERS, "HERE-AND-NOW" ATTITUDE

Bad Kid   Good Child

Level of instincts, emotions and feelings

BAD vs. GOOD

PLEASURE ORIENTED, HEDONISTIC, "SEX-MONEY-POWER" PRIORITIES, SELFISH, IMPULSIVE, AGGRESSIVE, POSSESSIVE, DEFIANT	CREATIVE, NAÏVE, INNOCENT, PLAYFUL, HELPFUL, WANTING EVERYBODY TO BE HAPPY, ALTRUISTIC, RECEPTIVE

Figure 2
CRITICAL PARENT
ACCEPTING PARENT
INDIFFERENT ADULT
COMPASSIONATE ADULT
BAD KID
GOOD CHILD

WHAT DOES LOVE-AND HATE- GOT TO DO WITH IT?

A LOT!

O.K., now we know that our psyche consists of six different modes.

Which mode has what for love & hate?

Positive Parent LOVES, unconditionally.

Positive Adult LIKES-for a given reason.

Positive Child FALLS IN LOVE-a gift.

Negative Parent HATES-conditionally.

Negative Adult DISLIKES-for a given reason.

Negative Child FALLS IN HATE-a curse.

Close your eyes... view all those people with whom you had/have an emotional relationships...evaluate your feelings for these people...think about those movie characters... do the same!

Not many people considered Gary Cooper a great actor. The author's ADULT has not found him powerful within that context. However, his CHILD adored him...He watches his hero's films again and again...His PARENT too, admired the old Coop for his stereotyped but steady movie characters that kept bringing decency and integration to the silver screen.

John Wayne was about the same... He portrayed, however, quite a brutish character in his representing what was GOOD and RIGHT for all of us in comparison to Gary Cooper's kind and reluctant variety. The writer's CHILD and PARENT celebrated him always while his ADULT found the acting very limited!

Regarding to Orson Welles, the author's CHILD was scared of him and his PARENT was not necessarily in agreement with this movie mogul's projects. However, his ADULT endorsed Orson's genius in acting, directing, writing, producing and all other movie industry jurisdictions. He was something!

The author's CHILD fell in love with Audrey Hepburn and PARENT was highly receptive to her "nice classy feminine lady" attitude. His ADULT, however, has never seen her portraying an evil character hence the question of versatile acting capability.

The writer never liked Bette Davis because of what his CHILD and PARENT observed. She, however, conquered his ADULT through her extremely versatile and beautiful acting! It has not been an easy job to portray a damsel in distress with whom we all sympathized and depicting narcissistic character in the next film with which we loved to hate her!

Those readers of the new generations may add their own list when they think about the contemporary actors and actresses.

In conclusion, the movies help us to sort out our feelings we have for others as well as ourselves in the real life hence the importance. After all, the feelings play important roles in our lives.

A MAN FOR ALL SEASONS: ONE ACTOR PLAYS ALL SIX MODES!

No doubt that many actors and actresses, especially the versatile ones, have already portrayed characters communicating with those three levels corresponding with our own infrastructure. The one the author keeps demonstrating for the educational as well as therapeutic purposes for years is Spencer Tracy (1900-1967).

This silver screen giant has depicted six different characterizations in six different movies corresponding to the six different modes we have already discussed.

He was Judge Heywood, chairing the judicial hearings staged for the trial sentencing German judges served under Hitler in the 1961 movie, *Judgement at Nurenberg*. His extreme conviction of what was right and wrong hence his decision in sentencing the judges to life in prison despite the powerful political overtures imposed on him to do otherwise was an excellent example of "Negative Parent" qualities. The scene showing his final chat with the German attorney portrayed by Maximillian Schell (Supporting Actor Oscar Award for his performance in the movie) is in a way chilling to watch when he says, "…yes, that may be logical -for those who have been sentenced to life being free in five years- but, being logical is not right…and nothing in the God's earth, makes it right!"

Remember right vs. wrong?

Spencer Tracy's characterization of the affluent father of Katherine Houghton in the 1967 movie, *Guess Who's Coming to Dinner* was an excellent example of the parental level of functioning; this time representing the other pole, "Positive Parent." Like *Judgement at Nurenberg*, again the other giants & giantesses of the silver screen surrounded him, Katherine Hepburn (the wife) and Sidney Poitier (the future son-in-law). The story centralizes around their daughter's decision to marry an African American doctor, and the parents' struggle to digest the whole matter related to interracial relations. At the end, while still in a critical, doubtful and disappointed state, he never-the-less accepts what has been going on and cautions the young couple while extending his blessings.

Remember acceptance?

The 1955 movie, *Bad Day at the Black Rock*, is the film where we watch him as a non-science fiction prototype of Schwarzenegger's Terminator! He portrays a fifties G-Man, sent out to the remote town to investigate the crime committed & covered by the regional goons. His one arm is literally afflicted and becomes the subject of teasing by the thugs. He, however, shows them that his one arm is enough "to tame down their belligerence!" He is issue centered, narrowly defined goal directed, a no-nonsense professional barely showing any affect throughout the movie! His performance corresponds to our "Negative Adult" modes!

Remember "Just the Facts, Ma'am?"

The Clarence Darrow characterization he demonstrates in the 1960 movie, *Inherit the Wind* is a depiction of the "Positive Adult" mode where what he does in the Judgment of Nuremberg is beautifully reversed! This time, he defends reason against the very powerful "Negative Parent" prosecutor played by Frederick March during the Scopes Monkey Trial of 1925! Unlike his adult character in "Bad Day at the Black Rock", he is compassionate, passionate, and demonstrates a lot of emotions and cares for everybody including his opposition.

Remember the problem solving, serving everybody's best interest?

Spencer Tracy as a "Bad Kid?" This was an interesting twist on the part of the producers' casting him as a corrupt, selfish and hedonistic chief of police in the eve of his imminent retirement after long decades of service with integrity! The 1963 movie, *It's Mad, Mad, Mad, Mad World!* is about a bunch of scavengers who are after a loot! This movie is a hilarious one as it shows how greed is able to turn otherwise law-abiding citizens into the belligerent sociopaths in quite a dark-comedy genre.

Remember the trigon of the devilish Bad Kid's "Sex-Money-Power" triangle?

Last but not least, this great actor played the "Good Kid" as well! The 1950 movie, *Father of the Bride*-no pun is intended, however-, casts him as a very nice individual who wants to make everybody happy during his daughter's wedding! He is anxious, panicky, creative, depressed, indecisive, dependent and cannot say "no" to anybody!

Remember, "let us all be happy?"

Now, relax and close your eyes... Do you remember your own films in which you were playing different characters relevant to the real life events?

WHICH PATIENTS ARE REFERRED TO MOVIE GROUP THERAPY?

The clinician expects the participants to demonstrate at least a moderately functioning mind enough to assimilate, process and resolve the issues through observation and discussion. Seriously and persistently mentally ill consumer population for example, may not necessarily be qualified for such a model as their minds, especially during the relapse, may not have capacity to grasp the messages, or at the other extreme, may grasp non-existent ones due to the morbidity of the emotional afflictions they have.

The writer has once shown a clip from the movie, *The Snake Pit* to his relatively stabilized persistently and severely mentally ill partial hospitalization patients. The rationale was comparing the way the state hospital residents have been treated in the past, to the actual treatment the partial care patients have received before their discharge from their respective hospitals in our contemporary time!

What was the result?

It was a disaster!

After a couple of minutes of show, some patients stood up and left with anger, some cursed, some became hysterical, tearful and shouted and still some others thought that the author was going to send them to THAT specific hospital!

The writer shared the same clips with high functioning groups as well. The members consisted of emotionally afflicted patients with relationship, employment, socio-familial and other psychosocial stress-inducing circumstances. Some were sympathetic with the movie heroine, some observed the good and bad clinicians, some offered a few clinical remedies and still some others were appreciative of having emotional problems in the nineties and not during those forties! The clips actually generated quite therapeutic discussions.

The other contraindication would be strong personality dispositions dominating and even compromising the group project.

The best approach for the movie therapist is interviewing his/her prospective clients and assessing their mental, emotional and spiritual capacities before including them in the group. Perhaps inviting each patient to visit the group for one session, with no charge-an attractive incentive relevant to the economical parameter-just to observe the style and format would be preferred. That may be very helpful for the therapist to decide whether the potential patient would be appropriate for the group formation and maintenance.

WHAT MAY BE THE THEMES FOR MOVIE GROUP THERAPY?

First, the answer is:

ANYTHING YOU CAN THINK OF!

Those traditional group therapy themes include but are not limited to

ANXIETY
DEPRESSION
POST TRAUMATIC STRESS DISORDER (PTSD)
EMPOWERMENT [WOMEN ***AND*** MEN]
EMOTIONAL INTENSITY/ANGER MANAGEMENT
ABUSE
ASSERTIVENESS TRAINING
COPING WITH CHRONIC/TERMINAL ILLNESS
CARETAKER GROUPS
WELLNESS/SUPPORT GROUPS

Second, there are "pearls" we would all like to know regardless of the type of those groups:

WHAT do we say or do when our loved one tells us that s/he has cancer?

HOW can we get out of the mess through humor especially those problems we inadvertently create?

WHO delivers the best help to a friend?

WHERE we can disarm the emotional furor of others?

WHEN do we need to heal the spirit if no cure for the body/mind is available?

These questions and some others necessitate special vignettes for discussion of the given matter relevant to special media, educational and therapeutic groups.

Third, other special relationship issues may also be easily addressed by group movie therapy such as EMPLOYER-EMPLOYEE (professional burn-out, workplace violence, teamwork, facilitating communication to increase revenues and etc.), INSTRUCTOR-STUDENT (group dynamics, teaching styles, student body dynamics, school violence and etc.), CLERGY-CONGREGATION (clergy burn-out, congregational dynamics, mental health issues and their spiritual resolution and etc.)

HOW DOES MOVIE GROUP THERAPY WORK?

The movie therapy is a kind of lab in which participants initialize, process, maintain and finish with the results (see Figure 3).

Of what?

Feeling, thoughts and beliefs, of course!

Most of the time we may not be aware of our INTRAPERSONAL relationships. There are six modes communicating among themselves for any given issue, situation or problem and its possible resolution. The movies and/or their clips provide the INTERPERSONAL media, the lab we have just mentioned, to facilitate, clarify and/or simplify the inner transactions for us to understand ourselves better.

How?

The group participants watch the commercial movie clip. They PROJECT their beliefs, thoughts and feelings on the actors & actresses portraying the characters. They IDENTIFY WITH or DISAVOW them. Then comes processing and problem solving, WORKING THROUGH on those characters' behalf. Once the results of problem solving suggestions are crystallized, the group INTROJECTS the whole process back to their own reality. The group moderator may ask the participants about their impression of what has been going on in the clip, what they would have been doing had they be in the shoes of those characters, alternative actions and all other thought stimulating questions. The participants' response and ideal discussion expected to take place among them reflect each individual's insight into their own difficulties for which they have been attending the sessions. Therefore, that VCR or the DVD turns out to be "a co-therapist/educator!" The best asset of such an approach is being educated and/or treated while entertained!

We do not forget the experience we have under two mutually exclusive extreme conditions:

Suffering and entertainment.

Who wants to suffer? We all do in any given day, anyway... This leaves us with the other extreme: Having fun!

...and that is where the movie group therapy steps in!

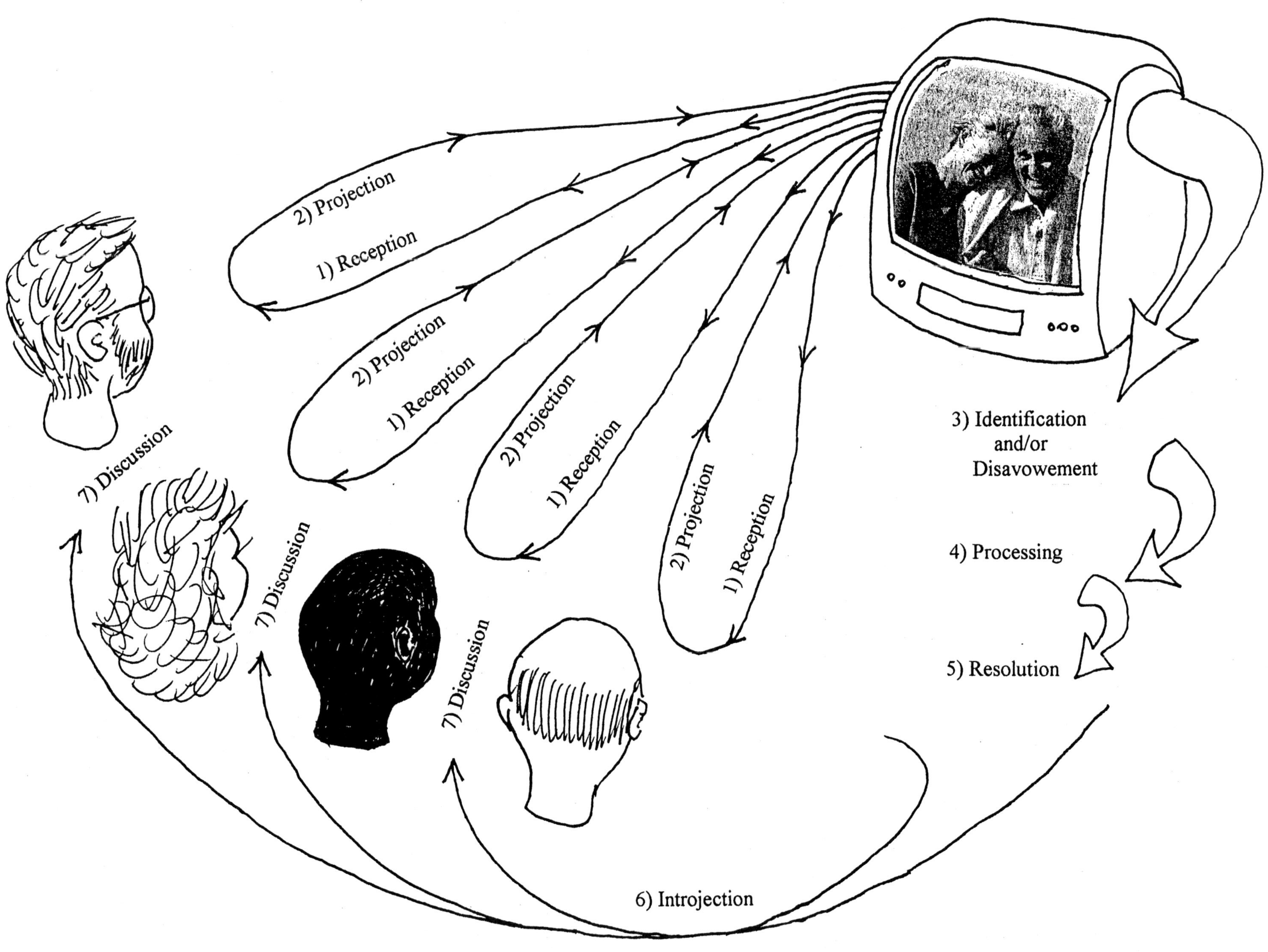

Figure 3
2) Projection
1) Reception
2) Projection
1) Reception
2) Projection
1) Reception
2) Projection
1) Reception
7) Discussion
7) Discussion
6) Introjection
3) Identification and/or Disavowement
4) Processing
5) Resolution

WHO CAN BE A MOVIE GROUP THERAPIST?

First, contact:

Motion Picture Licensing Corporation
5455 Centinela Avenue
P.O. Box 66970
Los Angeles, CA 90066-6970
Tel: (800) 462-8855
Tel: (310) 822-8855
Fax: (310) 822-4440
Web: www.mplc.com

They have a list of motion picture companies, e.g. MGM, Paramount, Universal and etc. Let them know the purpose of the public movie demonstration, i.e. education and/or treatment. They ask the inquirer to pay the annual fee for waiving the copyright laws regarding public presentation of the films produced by the companies on their list. They issue an annual license upon receiving the payment. The clinician displays this license in the premises where the group meetings are held.

Otherwise, the public usage of the tapes we own or rent violates the copyright laws.

The author personally has never heard of any instructor or therapist "violating" the copyright laws due to his/her using movie clips in the classrooms or therapeutic settings. Uncle Sam has been kind enough not to brutally reinforce this as He may welcome the education and/or treatment of His citizens. The copyright laws, however, are strictly enforced if we for example, make hundreds of copies of a given motion picture, sell them within the line of "piracy" and illegally profit made out of the process! It is also against the law to show a given commercial movie in the public with or without charging fees!

In conclusion, it is better to pay the annual fee and sleep comfortably thereafter!

Second, the cinema group therapist needs to be a bit of "movie buff!" S/he needs to know many movie scenes that are successfully used for the given theme(s).

Third, development and maintenance of insight relevant to "what to show to which group and when" is necessary on the part of given clinician. "Right subject for the wrong group in a questionable time period" may make things more complicated instead of facilitating the group dynamics! For example, showing suicide to depression groups, some members of which are well known-or worse, unknown- participants with history of a suicidal attempt (s) would be a terrible disservice! Sharing a morbid PTSD scene with the group, some members of which may not necessarily yet be working through their malady, may end up with an acting out creating a disaster, as well.

Fourth, the cinema group therapist needs to inform the members about the format each time before showing the given clip. The participants expect to watch and share those scenes hence the formation of the group in the first place. However, it is the clinician's ingenuity to decide what to show, where to stop, how to interpret and finally, how to figure out the process through which s/he monitors the group dynamics. The clips, when selected properly, are excellent stimuli for discussion starters. A novice cinema group therapist, therefore, may start with this simple idea in mind before extending him/herself to the other more innovative formats, such as stopping the clip and asking the participants to guess the next part of the vignette, asking the members to generate alternative scenes, role playing/psychodrama, and etc

HOW ABOUT PAYMENTS AND BILLINGS?

There is no problem for those therapeutic settings designed for inpatient, partial hospitalization and outpatient services as the facilities along with those agencies in charge of the program bill the services in the same way they do for any other group therapy. The billings, however, are to be reflective of the treatment theme. In other words, the insurance companies may reject reimbursements if they receive cinema/film/movie therapy "bills!" Kindly keep in mind that the rationale of such a therapy is not to educate, treat or heal the participants about "the movies." It is about PTSD, relationship issues, self-esteem, problem solving, anger management, depression, grief, anxiety, OCD and all other afflictions for which the patients seek help hence group therapy billing reflective of theme for which the patients get together.

The question, if we really need to address, relates to the private practitioners who would like to provide group movie therapy in the community. The average group therapist needs to authorize treatments through insurance companies. This process is not necessarily smooth, neither is it guaranteed in our contemporary HMO dominated mental health care era. It costs the practitioner unnecessarily wasting his/her time, energy and work, not to mention that reimbursements may be even lesser than the deductibles!

Since the given practitioner expects the clients to submit their co-payments or deductibles, the fee for group movie therapy may be paid through those channels without the authorization of the insurance companies. Eight people in the group will pay, for example, $15.00 per each session for six weeks. This makes $120.00 per session relevant to the therapist's compensation. It costs each patient $90.00 in total for six weeks attendance. Considering the simplicity, applicability and practicality-not to mention the education and entertainment-of the sessions with the real life problem solving potentials, many patients would be willing to afford this financial investment despite the economical recession we experience during the time of this writing.

Group therapy also provides a professional satisfaction for the psychiatrists. They have been misperceived as "the pill-pushers" in last decades when only fifteen minute "med-checks" have been authorized by the insurance companies, Medicare and/or Medicaid systems for their services. The psychotherapeutic treatment modalities have been delegated to the non-medical mental health providers. By the virtue of being physicians, the psychiatrists have been healers who would be seeking and applying all those healing tools to treat their patients. Group Movie Therapy gives this chance to the ones who are interested to practice psychiatry in the very way they were taught back in their residency years!

STAIRWAYS BEHAVIORAL HEALTH OUTPATIENT CLINIC
AND
MILCREEK COMMUNITY HOSPITAL
GROUP MOVIE THERAPY EXPERIENCE

Stairways Behavioral Health Outpatient Clinic, 2910 State Street, Erie, PA 16508, Tel: (814) 454-5686, website: http://www.stairwaysbh.org has been known to be the one and only Commonwealth of Pennsylvania facility where the group movie therapy has ever been provided for the patients during the time of this writing.

The official program started on January 14, 2003, and continued between 1:00 PM and 2:30 PM, on Tuesdays. The first group has been assessed to be fifteen people, taking into consideration that the actual participants would not be more than ten due to possible no shows. At the time of this writing, ten people did show up for the first session. Considering the terrible winter weather, this number was thought to be satisfactory. There were seven during the second session and eight during the third one while the cold and snow were continuing to pound the region.

The team originally designed these sessions as open-ended meetings with no termination date. In other words, the patients were expected to attend continuously as long as they benefit from the gatherings.

Different themes have been established for the each meeting, e.g. problem solving, anger management, self-esteem, relationship, anxiety, PTSD, depression, etc. within the sense of presenting samples to the patients.

Mark Davis, LSW, facility therapist who has also been in charge of initial intakes has been designated as a co-therapist. He was expected to complete group progress notes and process the documentation relevant to the billing process.

Each patient has been provided a brief review reflective of his/her rationale for participation and expectations of such a group before s/he has started to attend the gatherings. S/he has been scheduled to assess the effectiveness of the group at the end of the sixth week. Further treatment plans relevant to his/her group participation or termination has been based therefore on subjective reports by the patients and objective observations by the staff.

Transactional Analysis was established as the school of thought through which problem solving capacities and competencies of the patients are assessed. The participants appeared to be quite intrigued while having fun with the film clips.

Most of them felt relief to find out there would be six ways to evaluate their problems as well as they had the same amount of problem solving options.

It has been thought that such an initial and introductory format be retained for three months. Depending on the further requests of the patient population, the treatment team extended following recommendations:

1) The formation and maintenance of close-ended groups: The specific theme, e.g. PTSD is selected, and six to eight patients form the group for six weeks, at the end of which the group is dissolved and the new one starts.

2) Proportionate to the popularity of the treatment format and style, community expansion is expected. The clergy and congregations, law enforcement, courts, higher education, business, prison and all other compartments of the given community are contacted and marketing is promoted.

Partial hospitalization program has already been phased out in Erie County before the examiner's arrival in October 2001 and this type of therapeutic modality relevant to groups has been thought to be an excellent antidote to compensate for absence of such a treatment setting.

The Group Movie Therapy has also been considered for the inpatient setting, Behavioral Health Unit of Milcreek Community Hospital, 5515 Peach Street, Erie, PA 16509, in the region. Two psychiatric nurses, Kim Marsh, RN, BSN and Dawn Johnson, RN, BSN have shown interest in applying the modality especially during the weekends when the group activities would be minimal or limited. The author trained them within the line of Transactional Analysis and simple problem solving group theme identity was established. At the time of this writing, the said nurses started the program effective January 26, 2003 and continued on February 2 and 9, 2003.

The therapist with the minimal MA/MS qualifications, however, is required for charting as well as billing purposes relevant to such a service provided on the inpatient unit. The hospital officials are to be contacted in the near future if and when the said introductory therapy sessions become popular among the inpatient clients whose participations are indicated during their daily treatment plans.

Movietherapy

Stairways Behavioral Health

Outpatient Clinic

**Presents a New
Interactive Group!**

Starting January 7th
Time: 1:00 PM

Go to the Movies at Stairways!

Form and maintain Problem Solving Movie Groups.

Discuss the scenes with the therapists and your fellow group members.

Find solutions for problems seen in the films and draw parallels to real life.

Samples from Movie Clips Gallery

HANNAH AND HER SISTERS (1986)

Perhaps, Woody Allen's Hannah and Her Sisters has been the first film in which the movie therapy concept has ever been processed.

Woody, portraying one of his infamous hypochondriac-anxious-depressed-and in this film-suicidal characters, wants to commit suicide, as he doubts that God exists and does not want to live in the world without God hence no reason to go on.

He ends up going into the movie house without even watching the film. All he needs is to have rest so he can put things into perspective after a long and tiring walk.

Well, the movie is familiar to him-The Duck Soup-One of those Marx Brothers farces. Slowly but steadily, he starts to identify with the characters he watches on the screen. They are funny, jovial and full of life. Suddenly, a mini catharsis surfaces and he decides to live and enjoy the experience of life while he still can without necessarily being obsessed with the spiritual issues he may or may not comprehend!

EXISTENTIAL, SUPPORT AND EMPOWERMENT GROUPS

PSYCHODRAMA IN A BARN?

AGNES OF GOD (1985)

This is quite a disturbing, powerful, fascinating as well as controversial film that is very important for various reasons. In its entirety, it is the author's view that it is the best motion picture that ever been produced regarding the relationship among organized religion, spirituality and psychiatry. It has many clips that the clinician may share with the group participants for so many different issues.

Jane Fonda portrays a chain smoking court-appointed psychiatrist to examine Meg Tilly, depicting the nun who gets pregnant first and then allegedly kills the baby after birth in the convent. Anne Bancroft portrays Mother Superior of the facility. Three powerful performances make the movie superb!

The vignette shared with the psychodrama groups is the scene when the clinician approaches the nun who is completing her daily choirs in the barn. We understand that the nun is traumatized by her controlling and demeaning mother during her childhood. The psychiatrist offers to take over her mother role and each time encourages the nun to respond not with what she has to but in the very sincere way she feels. Jane Fonda starts demeaning her the way her mother has in the past and slowly but steadily, the nun's responses get more assertive and even aggressive.

Psychodrama in a barn?

You bet... and a good one too!

TARGET GROUPS: Psychodrama, PTSD, anxiety, depression, assertiveness and self esteem. Its presentation to the clergy, congregations and mental health groups is an excellent stimulator relevant to the debates staged for the given theme, i.e. organized religion vs. psychiatry, spirituality vs. behavioral sciences and etc.

THE RUNAWAY BUNNY!

WIT (2000)

Wow!

Prepare your handkerchiefs... This is a scary tearjerker!

Here, the tears fall due entirely to the health care realities of our contemporary time.

Emma Thompson portrays a higher education instructor who ends up having breast cancer. The worst of her problems, however, starts when she becomes the patient of highly specialized medical authorities of cancer management. From the chief of services to the resident physician rotating in the setting, she becomes a number! They regulate her treatment through checking the lab reports, while they do not even look at her during the examinations. In one scene, the resident physician shares his fascination with the cancer cells, while the patient before his very eyes endures side effects of the treatment! In another scene, she attempts to tell him about her anxieties, but the resident physician immediately asks her who the President of the United States is and offers a consultation to be provided by the other subspecialties probably psychiatry!

One needs to watch the movie in its entirety. However, the scene to be shared with the groups is at the end of the movie. Now, our patient is in morbid pain, tearful, agitated, sedated through medications, and is unexpectedly visited by her aged mentor. The old woman, on her way to join the grandchildren for a family festivity, wants to visit with her old student and is told about the condition hence her visiting with the patient in the hospital. She is terrified by the shape of her old pupil and after processing it for a few moments, she gets into her bed, puts her head on her lap, and starts reading her the book, The Runaway Bunny, as if she is reading it to her grandchild prior to her sleep time in the evening. This spiritual closeness, the tone of her voice and caring body contact leads Emma Thompson's characterto regress back to her childhood. Her mind is put at ease enough to start sleeping, her last sleep prior to passing away in the next couple of minutes...

The old mentor, realizing the patient's surrendering her soul, gently places the patient's head on the pillow, utters a few words reflective of a prayer, kisses her on the forehead, and leaves the bed and eventually the room as if nothing happened!

Wow, all right!

I cry every time I watch that scene.

The moral of this clip represents the difference between *curing* and *healing*!

Curing is the elimination of the disease through tangible-measurable-observable means including but not limited to medications, radiotherapy, chemotherapy, physiotherapy, surgery, etc. We may or may not be successful in doing so.

Healing, on the other hand, is promoting the well being of the spirit. It is a promotion of the afflicted person's soul into a peaceful setting...Peace with herself and others in this vignette. It is uplifting the spirit into the level where the patient, despite her agony, learns to live with the problem, and accepts it as it is.

The doctors were supposed to be "the healers" a long time ago... Unfortunately, their practice in our contemporary times have been compromised by many non-medical interferences such as insurance company authorizations, malpractice crisis due to frivolous cases, government regulations, inadequate reimbursements and undue reliance on the advanced technology replacing the bedside manners. The doctors have been under pressure leading them to spend less place and time during the suffering displayed by their patients. This movie presents this dilemma very realistically.

The patient whose mind cannot be put at ease through the expertise of many specialists for months, finds healing provided by the old mentor within five minutes, comforted enough to find peace in her death!

TARGET GROUPS: Caretakers, support groups for medically and surgically afflicted patients, terminal patients and/or their families, medical student and resident physician education, coping groups.

SLAPPING EACH OTHER AND…THEN, *WHAT?*

RULES OF THE MARRIAGE (1984)

Here is my best clip for the relationship groups in general and family therapy in particular.

Elliott Gould and the late Elizabeth Montgomery portray a married couple. Once being in love, they slowly but steadily distance themselves from each other in the later phase of their ten year old union; both have affairs with some others and come to the terms of discussing divorce.

The scene starts with Liz's bringing their two children to visit with their dad who has already separated himself from them. She wants to talk to him before they finalize the details. The children are asked to play outside of the beach house and she takes over, starts talking to him.

The next twenty minutes is one of the best examples of Transactional Analysis, as both are engaged in the conversation alternatively displaying child-to-parent, adult-to-adult, adult-to-child, parent-to-adult, parent-to-parent and so on so forth.

Somehow, their discussion turns into argument and the argument turns into the verbal fight leading their slapping each other while they converse on the child-to-child plane!

The author usually stops the clip and asks the group to guess what is to happen in the next scene.

No one has guessed it yet!

The writer himself could not either when he saw the movie for the first time!

They stop for a moment bewildered by the their physical aggression not knowing what to do next!

They start laughing histrionically enough to double up, falling to the floor!

Once they are through, we see them communicating to each other within the line of adult-to-adult until the scene ends. Both decide that they need to stay together, provided both of them would be comfortable, safe and secure with each other.

It is NOT necessarily, "a goody-two-shoes happy ending" at all. They realize now that there are things they can do as well as they cannot in the marriage, but the essence of their agreement is to be safe with each other, enough to let the other know what exactly the one feels, thinks and believes…well, just like two adults!

TARGET GROUPS: Relationship, emotional intensity and family therapy.

IS WHAT IS LOGICAL,
A) RIGHT?
B) WRONG?
C) NEITHER?

JUDGEMENT AT NURENBERG (1960)

I did not want to see the remake of this movie on purpose. They say that its production, direction and acting have been superb. The original however, has been so powerful, thus leading me to end up with disappointment if I see the remake regardless of its quality...The old black & white production still sends chills to my spine despite my seeing the film for more than twenty times!

The scene I share with the groups is at the end of the movie.

Spencer Tracy, portraying Judge Heywood, the chief of the US tribunal, passing life sentences to the German judges served under the Third Reich, prepares to leave for home following the conclusion of the hearings. He is visited by Counselor Rolfe, portrayed by Maximillian Schell (Best Supporting Actor Oscar for his performance), asking him to visit with his client Judge Jannings depicted by Burt Lancaster (The author has always liked him with his "killer smile and laughter" presented in those action movies. Here, however, he is superb in his aging make-up portraying an elderly and a tragic character with German accent!) who wants to see him before he leaves for the US. Judge Heywood reluctantly agrees.

Counselor Rolfe in the meantime offers him a gentleman's wager, that all of those four German judges sentenced to life in prison would be free in five years!

Judge Heywood looks at him, bitterly smiles and extends his commendations for Counselor Rolfe's brilliant defense using reason and logic during the hearings. He affirms that given the political climate of the contemporary international politics, the counselor's speculation may be LOGICAL and yes, they may be set free within five years. He, however, adds with a chilling sensation that, "What is logical is not RIGHT... Nothing on God's earth may make it RIGHT!"

Well, those of you who answered the title multiple choice quiz with "D" are the winners!

Yes, one is not to mix the Parental level "Right vs. Wrong" with the Adult functioning emphasized by "Logical vs. Illogical."

Most people have difficulties as they may not be aware of their misidentifying "Right" with "Logical Choice" during any given debate, discussion or argument. The participants need to identify these two distinct levels before proceeding further if they are transmitting messages within the different frequencies!

TARGET GROUPS: Relationship, assertiveness and problem solving groups.

BUT I DID TRY, DIDN'T I, GOD DAMN IT? ...LEAST, I DID THAT!

ONE FLEW OVER THE CUCKOO'S NEST (1975)

This movie did a terrible disservice to the mental health profession and the people who seek help for emotional affliction. Its indeed reflecting some misuse if not the abuse of treatment witnessed in the archaic times of the institutionalization of the earlier decades, the film in general and the application of Electro Convulsive Treatment (ECT) in particular were not yet erased from people's mind for more than a quarter of the century.

We provide this treatment selectively and quite safely in our contemporary time but the stigma attached to application continues to be a problem.

Nevertheless, the movie also has some important scenes about the patients and their struggles.

There are so many vignettes in this film where one can share the scenes with various groups for different reasons. The one I will be mentioning here is the clip where McMurphy, portrayed by Jack Nicholson, expresses his intentions of picking up the terribly heavy water fountain base, throwing it towards the barred windows, running out of the hospital, going to downtown, and watching the ball game in one of the bars! His fellow inmates raise the question of his credibility regarding what he claims to do, i.e. picking up the fountain base. He bets he is going to do it and challenges them to offer a wager. A few of them bet from a dime to $25.00 that he would not be able to do it!

Well, of course, after trying very hard not only once but twice, he quits. Dejected and frustrated, he verbalizes the famous phrase while passing through before them in returning to his room, "...but I did try, didn't I, God damn it...least I did that!", insinuating their idle and inept behavior; in not doing anything for the mistreatment they all receive on the unit.

This scene leads to discussion for two reasons.

First, it shows how "trying" is important for the people in general and the men in particular as most males do not want to try but do it. Trying helps us to get rid of the guilt or shame and generates us the factual reason for which we would promote our self-esteem. Excuses lower our spirit and make incompetent creatures out of us. The Adult level of functioning necessitates our execution of trying and once we do, we have no further excuses for failure even we fail what we try to accomplish.

Second, one's trying and failure may still inspire others to try. This is exactly what happen in the movie. The tall, big and so-called "deaf-and-dumb" American Indian, befriending McMurphy, does the very same at the end of the picture and he succeeds hence escaping the institution, fulfilling the title of the movie!

TARGET GROUPS: Men's Empowerment Groups

GO AHEAD... MAKE MY DAY!

SUDDEN IMPACT (1979)

Here is the phrase, the chapter title, epitomized by Clint Eastwood's Dirty Harry Callahan character!

Now, you will ask what on an earth Dirty Harry has anything to do with group therapy...

A LOT!

Harry coincidentally interferes with the coffee-shop robbery carried out by four thugs. He shoots them down, one by one, and the last thug, wounded, takes a waitress hostage while Callahan approaches him. The robber points his gun to his hostage's head giving Harry a message, "You intend to get me and I will harm her!"

Instead of complying with this threat, Harry continues to point his gun at him and snarls, "Go ahead ... make my day!"

His counter-message is, "Do to her whatever you want so I may have an excuse to get you!"

The perpetrator thinks for a moment, quits and surrenders to the police who have already arrived at the location.

The insight here is reviewing our capacity to fight fear, leading us to avoid situations inducing anxiety, panic and/or phobia. Behavioral Modification therapists apply desensitization, relaxation training, paradoxical intention, flooding and all other tools to help their clients to "neutralize" their fears in a systematic discipline. The most important step, however, is our ability to call the fear's bluff, saying, "Go ahead, make my day!"

We need to face our fears... Once we figure that out, we realize that it is not as morbid as we think it is.

Some deny the representation of something therapeutic in this clip. However, despite high incidence and prevalence of anxiety, panic and/or phobia we witness in our society, there have not been many productions clips of which may be alternative sources!

TARGET GROUPS: Anxiety, fear and phobia groups.

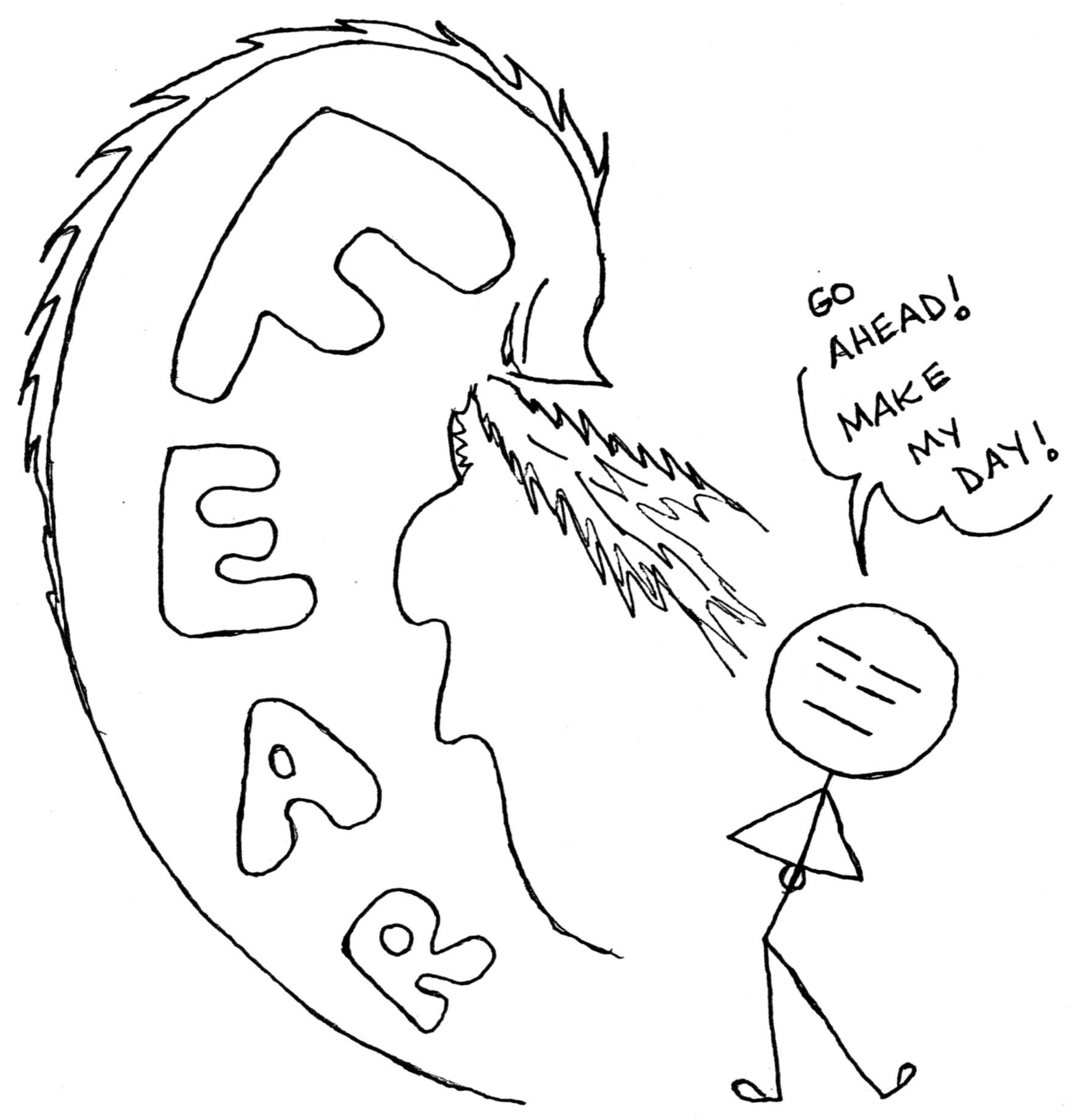
FEAR
GO AHEAD! MAKE MY DAY!
WHEN DID YOU AVOID YOUR FEAR?
WHEN DID YOU FACE IT?
WHAT HAD HAPPENED?

ONE WORD, MANY MESSAGES!

THE BRIDGE ON THE RIVER KWAI (1957)

This vignette is an excellent example of one word's multiple messages!

It is WW-II and we are in the Allies POW camp governed by the Japanese... The camp commander orders the POWs to build a bridge vital to the Japanese... Alec Guinness, portraying the POW chief opposes the circumstances that his men became subject to and asks his terms to be established first before any work is expected of the POWs. His Japanese counterpart refuses and makes Alec's character subject to receiving terrible torture. It is the battle of wills however and the British commander wins, the Japanese chief accepts the terms, and The British commander gives **his word** to build and preserve the bridge...

Meanwhile Bill Holden portraying an American officer escapes from camp and returns with the commandoes targeting to hit the bridge before the Japanese start transporting men and war material. The shoot out starts, but we see Alec's character dumbfounded, anxious, agitated and confused, trying to do his best to counter the attack!

He is wounded and suddenly comes face to face with Bill Holden's character who has also been wounded. Alec says, "You?" in a crescendo tone, extending messages such as, "I thought you were dead... Why are you here? Why are you here? Are you responsible for this raid? Why? Don't you know I gave **my word** to preserve this bridge?"

Bill looks at him in disgust and he too, verbalizes the same word, "You!" except in a decrescendo mode sending messages such as, "You old you-know-what... Why are you trying to fight against your own people? Is your word more important than the tide of war being turned against our enemy? Go to hell!"

Both slump and die while the bridge is blown to pieces...

This scene always generates lively discussion when the group is asked about the messages carried by the same word verbalized by two different people. The group members learn to read the messages of those monosyllable responses and their importance in enhancing meaningful conversations.

RELATIONSHIP AND PROBLEM SOLVING GROUPS

TRY THESE WORDS TO EXPRESS YOUR FEELINGS:

SURE...

WHY?

I SEE...

GOD...

YES...

NO...

I DON'T KNOW...

GREAT...

$$\text{“I WANT MY COFFEE IN A CUP!”}$$

KISS TOMORROW GOODBYE (1950)

Humor, especially when used properly, is not only good for the spirit-mind-body but also saves the neighborhood most of the times!

In this movie, James Cagney portrays one of his stereotyped gangster characters. The scene we are interested in watching here is his dialogue with his jealous girl friend portrayed by Barbara Peyton, who is the sister of one of his fellow inmates from the state penitentiary. Jimmy, while continuing to carry on with his "business-as-usual" has his eyes on the commissioner's daughter, a naïve beauty portrayed by Helena Carter. He sees her as another step on the social ladder on which he keeps going up, and thus he starts to think of getting rid of Barbara. In the said scene, we watch Jimmy joining the breakfast prepared by Barbara. She is very upset, knowing about him having a date with Helena. Jimmy, on the other hand, denies everything in a matter of fact style and claims he has been at a movie! Barbara's patience is exhausted, and she throws a coffee pot at him! He ducks and instead of getting angry, he tells her that he wants his coffee in a cup! She throws a cup and he ducks again. He asks for cream, and now cream goes sailing on the air! After another successful ducking, he asks for the sugar, and that too is thrown. At last, he says, "no cigar!", starts laughing, turns his back and sits on the couch, still laughing! This magically takes all the frustration off of Barbara's shoulders and she starts laughing as well. She approaches him, places herself on top of him while both are on the coach and warns him that one of these days she would have him be killed! He answers with the same dark humor that there is no cop in the world who would be shooting that straight. She adds that she does not mean a cop but she, herself! He continues teasing her, thinking that she is a law-abiding citizen! Her answer wraps around that she can be anything he wants her to be except sharing him with another woman! He playfully assures that he still does not know what she is talking about. He, after all, barely handles her, let alone another woman!

Sometimes, the humor, even in the dark variety, saves the day.

This clip is also good to discuss especially for the professionals, why the women with Borderline Personality traits get involved with the men with Antisocial Personality characteristics!

TARGET GROUPS: Humor therapy, relationship and problem solving groups.

TELL US YOUR BEST JOKE!

WHO FORGIVES THE GOD FOR THE HOLOCAUST?

THE QUARREL (1991)

This movie has many scenes that may be shown to different groups for various reasons. The one to be mentioned here is about our capacity to help emotionally afflicted people in that very moment they need the help most.

Yes, it is about "being with the people" during their emotional suffering...

What is "being with the people?"

Professionals and the loved ones alike, many individuals attempting to comfort the sufferer often end up with one of three approaches, none of which is desirable or healthy for the person who needs support:

1) Minimizing: "...Well, I understand you have cancer, but it can be worse and you would be dead by now..."

2) Patronizing: " ...You would not be able to handle this pain in any other way... I
Know how you feel... It is not easy..."

3) Criticizing: " ...You should have listened to me...I told you so...not to smoke your lungs to death..."

Most of the time, we feel obligated to do and/or say something in comforting the afflicted hence the motto: "Just don't stand there... Do something!"

Well, guess what? This is the situation where we need to reverse the said motto: "Just don't do something... Stand there!"

Be with the person...

This movie is about Hersh and Chaim, two dear friends whose relationship goes back to their student years in Yeshiva, the Jewish religious school in Byalestock, Poland in the eve of the World War II. Chaim drops out, wanting to be a writer and see the world. Hersh stays behind and becomes a rabbi. Both lose their families during the Holocaust while speculating that the other one too, is probably dead. Coincidentally, they meet in Montreal, Canada years later. Hersh is in a process of building his Yeshiva there while Chaim happens to be visiting the city for the conference he wants to attend. Following their getting over the first shock of seeing each other unexpectedly, the two poor souls start walking in the park, talk, sometimes laugh, sometimes bitter, bringing old memories into their conversation. Chaim is greatly angry to God for His "abandonment of the Jews" during the terrible times while Hersh defends Him, finding the faults in the Jews for their sins instead. The whole movie develops into a very emotionally charged debate between two old friends hence the title of the movie, *The Quarrel.*

After exhausting each other with their mutually alternating comfort and criticism, they open their hearts to each other. We find out that both men have the additional guilt problems regretting the things they have done or not done for their family members who vanished in the Holocaust. In Chaim's case, he feels guilty for not joining his family while being aware that the Germans were rounding up the village in which they lived while he was away from the region for his trade. He escapes to Siberia and returns back to whatever is left following the end of the war. He gets extremely tearful, starts crying and begs for his loved ones' forgiveness while both men sit on the bench. Hersh who happens to be very critical of Chaim for many reasons during the movie, looks at him, nods his head in sorrow, slumps over, brings the side of his body in touch with his dear friend, and stays as such. Now, he "is with his buddy."

The connection of this spiritual collectiveness clears their minds and allows them to recall the chant performed by one of their teachers in the school years ago. They desperately try to remember that during the movie but fail due to their emotionally charged states. Hersh starts to chant, Chaim complements it and what they do next is both dancing while uttering the chant.

This is called, "Regression in the service of ego" in psychiatry. It is a mature defense to avoid the pain through getting back to the time when the person has no affliction. Here, they productively regress into the times when they were innocent students with optimistic ideals before their disillusionments with the world.

TARGET GROUPS: Support, PTSD, relationship and emotional intensity groups. This is also great film for debates staged relevant to "free will" vs. "predetermination."

WHEN YOU HAVE TO SHOOT, SHOOT…DON'T TALK!

THE GOOD, THE BAD AND THE UGLY (1966)

Eli Wallach portraying Tuco (the Ugly) notices a wooden bathtub during his search in the abandoned building while the Civil War rages around the location. He starts humming and prepares for the bath. One of his nemeses, however, has been on his heels for weeks and spots him entering the building. He sneaks in and kicks the door of the bathroom while Tuco is caught off balance, water in the bath on his shoulders, looking helplessly at the intruder.

The person was apparently in a gunfight with Tuco months ago when his right hand was wounded, forcing him to practice with his left while he was looking for Tuco regarding his revenge. He starts to talk about how he was in pain; it was difficult for him to practice with his left, blah, blah blah… He finally aims and while everybody expects him to pull the trigger, Tuco is the one to shoot him with the six-shooter he has been keeping under the soap & water, the old tradition in the Wild West where you never let go of your gun regardless of where you are!

It takes a couple of shots to kill his opponent and when it is over, he utters the infamous statement with the indifference of a hardening bandit, "When you shoot, shoot…don't talk!"

This clip is good for the discussion when one needs to talk the talk AND walk the walk. It is of course not intended to encourage, "Shoot first and ask the questions later!" On the contrary, it emphasizes that "the walk" is to be complimentary to "the talk."

The individuals who "talk" about their intentions to quit smoking "next day", the people who plan to start dieting after the given festivity, the drug & alcohol abusers who feel that they can quit anytime they want, those "status quo" workers who do not want to "upset the apple cart" and all others that are not able to turn their words into the deeds benefit from the conversation stimulated by this short clip.

TARGET GROUPS: Relationship, motivation, substance abuse and business groups.

WHEN YOU NEED TO
TALK,
ooo TALK!

DON'T WALK!

BUT...
WHEN YOU NEED TO
WALK,
ooo WALK!

DON'T TALK!

I LOVE MY PATIENT!

LOVESICK (1983)

Dudley Moore, portraying a psychiatrist, ends up falling in love with one of his patients in this comedy flick!

So what?

Well, the clip showing him fantasizing about a romance with his newly assigned patient depicted by Elizabeth McGovern, is able to generate good discussions among the professionals and public alike. It is a harmless movie in the perspective that Dudley's character is really in love with his patient, and does not portray a predator sexually harassing the client in those real life stories and fictitious literature alike! He compromises his career knowing the boundary expectations, even sacrificing it just to be with her.

The audience in general, of course sides with admiring him while the professionals curse him in dishonoring his sacred trade. Alec Guinness is great playing Sigmund Freud's ghost, popping up from time to time, providing him with some Adult level of problem solving alternatives!

TARGET GROUPS: Relationship, ethics, doctor-patient contact discussions and debates.

I HATE MY PATIENT!

ANALYSE THIS (2000)

Have you ever said one thing while having an urge to say something entirely different but could not?

That moment is burn out!

Long years ago, one of my supervisors in psychiatry told me that if I wanted to say/do something but would not able to and instead had to say/do entirely the opposite of the originally imposing entity, that would be the sign of burn out, hence my need for the vacation!

Billy Crystal, portraying a psychiatrist, burnt out & needing a vacation, sees his histrionic patient depicted by Molly Shannon. Apparently, she has been going on and on for a while about her husband who filed a PFA on her! She, however, constantly asks her doctor what she should do...

We watch, with terrifying confusion while Billy's character starts to demean her, stands up, escalates his verbal attacks and finally shouts at her, "Get a f****** life!"

While we struggle with what we observe, suddenly the scene changes back to where Molly asks the question related to what she needs to do. Billy returns with a kind and gentle psychodynamic explanations where we gather that the previous scene is only acted out on his mind! He wants to do that but cannot...instead hides behind the professionalism!

TARGET GROUPS: Emotional intensity, burn out and relationship groups.

INTENSE COMMUNICATION WITH NO WORDS!

YOL/THE ROAD (1981)

This Turkish film which depicts psychosocial traditions and their impact on any given individual has a scene demonstrating haunted non-verbal communication, carried out even under tremendously stressful occasions.

The smugglers who are outlawed by the states on both sides of the border end up in a shootout with the National Guard forces. Those killed are placed in an open cart and displayed among the peasants for proper identification. All the villagers are asked to line up, go around the cart, view the dead bodies and inform those known ones to the officials.

Among the peasants, there is an old man concerned about the fate of his smuggler son. He asks one of his other sons to line up and view the bodies. His son who himself has been on a week pass from the minimal security prison, lines up, walks and looks at the cart. His stoic expression does not change even a bit. The audience too, at this point, cannot tell whether his brother is among the killed smugglers. He follows the other peasants, comes face to face with his father whose expression is as stoic as his own. These two men look at each other for a few moments and both the old man and the movie audience figure out that their loved one is indeed in the cart! The length of the mutual stare reflects the fact that the smuggler is dead... Once he gives this powerful non-verbal message to his father, continues to walk with the other peasants while not giving a clue to any officials observing the villagers.

RELATIONSHIP GROUPS

DOCTOR-PATIENT ROLE REVERSAL IN THE OFFICE...

DUET FOR ONE (1986)

Julie Andrews portrays a violinist who suddenly develops Multiple Sclerosis in the height of her career. Depression and anxiety force her to seek, however reluctantly, counseling. Max Von Sydow depicts her psychiatrist.

We learn that he has always adored her on the stage. Her scheduling an appointment through her husband intrigues the counselor.

She immediately discloses her condition while he is still in the phase of pleasantry to make her comfortable in the office during the first session. The information spilled acutely catches him off guard! He puzzles for a few moments, stands up, takes a few steps towards his bookshelf, and changes the places of couple of items without any purpose!

She expects him to take over and even uses dark humor to put his mind at ease!

It is a short clip but tells us about our Achilles Heel. We, after all, are human beings and would be as much surprised, as any other layman/woman when we are caught off balance, if especially the person in question is somebody we like, love or adore.

This clip is important for therapists and patients alike. It shows that the healers too, have feelings and the given problem of their afflicted fellow human beings may affect them. Many patients appreciate observing this.

The movie in its entirety is quite controversial however. We observe Max Von Sydow's character shifting from the role of the healer to the friend who provides great comfort to the performer in the last stages of her malady. This itself stimulates quite a good discussion among the group relevant to ethics.

TARGET GROUPS: Relationship, anxiety and ethics groups.

DO THERAPISTS LEARN FROM

THEIR PATIENTS ?

WHAT ?

HOW ?

ON WHAT ISSUE(S) ?

"OLD BLOOD 'N' GUTS" BEING A THERAPIST FOR ANXIETY?

PATTON (1971)

One of my all time favorites, George C. Scott portraying General Patton, delivers his speech to his troops in the beginning of the movie and continues as follows:

"I know you boys are wondering whether you will be chicken out under fire...Don't worry about it... I can assure you that you all are going to do your duty... Nazis are the enemy... Spill their guts... Shoot them in the belly... When you put your hand...on a bunch of goo... which was your best friend's face a moment ago...*you know what to do!*"

General Patton inadvertently comes up with a few behavioral and anthropological facts in his reassurance!

First, yes, fear is the mother of all negative emotions in the animal kingdom. (Some of the psychological orientations may not necessarily agree with that but what is being discussed is the way one feels during the battle!)

Second, it is fear that determines our fight or flight.

Third, anger, once it substitutes fear, may even be used for constructive purposes under the supervision of reason, in the line of Patton's mentality, winning the battle!

In other words, Transactional Analysis wise, we may use our BAD KID for the GOOD REASON!

TARGET GROUPS: Emotional intensity, anger, anxiety and panic groups.

SPEAK SOFTLY AND CARRY A BIG STICK!

MILLER'S CROSSING (1990)

Here we go again with another epitomized phrase, this time coined by Theodore Roosevelt... Mr. President was perhaps the master of some sort of adult level approach as what he had advised almost a century ago has been "alive and kicking" in the therapeutic circles!

The scene is in the beginning of the picture. John Torturro, portraying the Italian faction of the underworld visits with Albert Finney, depicting the Jewish Mafia Boss. He seeks Albert's blessings regarding the prospective hit on a double crossed bookie. The bookie's sister, on the other hand is wooed by both Finney and his henchman portrayed by Gabriel Bryne, hence their disagreement with this plan.

Albert does not give his blessings and further, warns John not even to think about it. John acutely loses it, starts shouting, standing up, and puts his hands on Albert's table, menacing while also agitating himself.

Albert's response to this is as cool as ever. Quietly but firmly he "reminds" him that it was he, Albert who brought John to his present level of power and he is not to forget it!

This cool, quiet but firm reminder forces John to disarm, compose himself, regain his previous demeanor and slowly retreat, leaving the room with his bodyguard accompanying him while mumbling and still expressing his disappointment.

The message?

We would be able to get the message across quicker and more efficient way if we would be quiet but firm... Mutual shouting contest and ever escalating agitation loses the issue we want the other party to be aware of.

TARGET GROUPS: Relationship, assertiveness and anger management groups.

WE DON'T NEED TO TRUST EACH OTHER... WE ARE DOING BUSINESS!

SCAM (1993)

These are the words of Christopher Walken who portrays a con man, verbalized to Lorraine Bracco who portrays a con woman in this "scammed" movie. The picture itself is a good one, and not many people would be able to guess the end accurately.

The scene shows the con woman entering the room of Christopher's character and asking him whether he can be trusted (the duo has been preparing a sting operation planned for others along with the possibility and probability for each other!). She further inquiries to see whether he, trusts her! The con man, in quite an indifferent, matter-of-fact style, tells her that they do not need to trust each other, as they are to be doing business. He further adds that if she indeed needs to trust something, she needs to trust the $5K he already has provided for her as "down payment" for her role in this whole deal!

This clip regardless how short and simple it may be, generates a great discussion especially in the business groups leading to the debate about the importance of trust among the business partners.

One one hand, trust is necessary for one to establish business with the other. The writer specifically asks the couples whom the author treats to look at their relationship through the business angle, i.e. what they individually invest and what kind of return they expect back...

On the other hand, trust is not necessarily an ADULT level of functioning. It is the product of CHILD and PARENT level relationships while we grow up. Therefore, the question may be asked whether the given parties need trust provided they have already been assured of their "returns", hence the credibility of the statement, i.e. "trust the $5K I gave you for the down payment of your services!"

Again, applying this to relationship theory, many "happy" marriages have not necessarily been built on trust but let us say security. I do remember a lot of women being in the marriage by the virtue of safety and comfort rather than the privilege of trust they maintain for their spouses. By the virtue of the same perspective, husbands too, may be happy having "comforting mothers" back in home while the trust again may not be an issue!

The clip stimulates the business groups as well. Some leaders may know how to promote their business while the staff may not necessarily trust them. S/he may not trust the staff either but keeps quiet as long as the business is well done!

TARGET GROUPS: Relationship and business groups

THE LONGEST DAY (1962)

Richard Beymer, portraying a lost GI desperately wanting to join any of the US companies, ends up in a French village following D-Day. He sees a German official lumped over the wall and approaches him with caution. Suddenly, a voice, "He's dead" is heard from nowhere, leading the GI to jump and hide. Well, here is Richard Burton, portraying a RAF pilot, badly wounded and sitting before the porch!

He further adds, "He was going to get me…but-he picks up his revolver and almost proudly adds-I got him!"

He asks the Yank to give him a cigarette, and these two soldiers are engaged with a buddy conversation as if they know each other for years…The RAF pilot smiles bitterly and says, "Funny isn't it? He is dead-shows the killed German-, I am crippled and you are lost… I suppose that's the way it happens…in war, I mean…"

This is one of the most beautiful examples for the indifferent adult self. Remember, "Well, that's the way it is" orientation? The factual and yet cold presentation of "Negative Adult Self?"

Keep in mind that this is also one of the defense mechanisms through which we protect ourselves from overwhelming stress. It may not be healthy, but it is definitely necessary at times. Richard Burton's character demonstrates that.

PROBLEM SOLVING GROUPS

…OR IS IT?

WHAT DO YOU THINK
WE CAN CHANGE?

WHAT DO YOU THINK
WE CAN TRY TO
CHANGE?

WHAT CAN NOT BE
CHANGED?

ASSERTIVE CHAT IN... THE MILITARY?

BATTLE OF THE BULGE (1964)

Assertion is not known in the military... The orders are given, taken, obeyed, disobeyed but... assertion?

Interestingly, one of the rare assertive dialogues that happen between the two soldiers shows us that in the military too, assertion at times produces better results than aggression.

Colonel Hessler, portrayed by the late Robert Shaw, one of my favorites, underrated actors, is given a spearhead commission in the counter-attack unexpectedly prepared against the Allies in the late Fall,1944. Despite his exhaustion generated by one hopeless battle after the other, he is excited for his new post and hopes that Germany has not yet been finished. The scene shows him having dinner and inviting his petty officer, long time friend to join him having a glass of wine. He feels that his petty officer has something in mind but is reluctant to verbalize it. He encourages him to speak his mind, the truth. After all, he feels-and smiles- that there should be some around him to tell him the truth!

His officer expresses his concerns over whether this new command would be an illusion! He wants his superior to give it up. The Colonel asserts himself that the military objectives achieved by his leading the armored divisions to victory at France, Poland and Crimea has NOT been an illusion. The Tiger Tank Brigade provided for the said attack in the Ardennes IS therefore a reality. Encouraged by the Colonel's sincerity, the petty officer further reminds him that all the veteran soldiers with whom he achieved his objectives are killed or gone. He asks him how he is going to be sure of the capability of his new staff leading tanks into the battle! Colonel looks at him, dumbfounded by his not necessarily considered this previously, and orders his brigade tank commanders to line up at once to find out the merit of his petty officer's concern!

Assertiveness is defending one's own belief, thought or feeling WITHOUT putting down other people because of their having different beliefs, thoughts or feelings. As this vignette shows, this achieves success all the time, while the aggressive, "My way or... the highway" attitude may automatically eliminate any possible and probable resolutions for the given problems.

TARGET GROUPS: Assertiveness, empowerment, relationship and coping groups.

TELL US YOUR LAST ASSERTIVE COUNTER !

AGGRESSIVE ONE ?

BOOZING UP, DOC?

THE HOSPITAL (1971)

Yes, here we go with the good old George G. Scott, again!

In this movie, he portrays the Chief of Medicine of the big, urban hospital. He has been depressed, drinking and smoking himself to death, abandoned by his wife, discarded by his children, staying in a hotel room, and displaying the text-book signs and symptoms of professional burn out!

The hospital CEO advises him to see the facility's psychiatrist after a few associates report to the office their concern about the Chief's contemplation of suicide. He refuses first but reluctantly barges into his colleague's office later on.

This is one of the most controversial psychiatric interviews I have ever observed in my 31 years of psychiatric experience.

The psychiatrist is quite an aloof professional who analyzes his colleague's troubles through a Negative Adult philosophy in this clip. We do not observe much mood or affect in his relationship with the troubled Chief of Medicine. The audience celebrates his competency in formulation and diagnosis while rebukes his extreme coldness, not showing even an inch or ounce of compassion!

Sharing this clip with the physician assistants, resident physicians, nurses, medical students and the different media groups, produces the same fascinating outcome of "debatable discussion" all the time: Half of the participants think that the assessment is awful while the other half of the attendants believe that it is a brilliant management!

Keep in mind that the identified patient here is a physician!

TARGET GROUPS: Depression, assertiveness and relationship groups.

HAVE YOU EVER HANDLED ANY CRISIS?

WHAT DID YOU DO?

COULD YOU DO ANY BETTER?

JUDD HIRSCH, MY ALL TIME FAVORITE MOVIE SHRINK!

THE ORDINARY PEOPLE (1980)

Judd Hirsch is casual, unpretentious, down the earth but no-nonsense shrink and Timothy Hutton (Best Supporting Actor Oscar for that year) is a depressed and suicidal adolescent.

Donald Sutherland portrays Tim's concerned but inept father, while Mary Tyler Moore depicts his cold and detached mother.

The real star of the movie, however, is the director: Robert Redford! He got the Best Director Oscar Award for his directorial debut for that year.

The film has also won the Best Picture and the Best Screenwriter Oscar awards as well.

The older brother of Tim's character dies in a boat accident. The mom detaches herself from Tim, blaming him for what happened, The dad desperately wants to be a peace maker in the family, and Tim tries to commit suicide, he is treated and referred to Judd's character for follow up.

There are six sessions in the movie, from the one sharing their first encounter to the resolution of Tim's problems during the final office visit. The brilliance of Redford and those two great actors make each session interesting to watch, independently from the sequential order. Each visit depicts about 5-10 minute portion of the whole hour session and generates a thought provoking discussion among the group therapy members. All visits have one thing in common: The shrink approaches his patient not necessarily through the cold and detached psychoanalytical perspective but common sense! He expresses passion for this adolescent while promoting slowly but steadily effective emotional insight in him, eventually helping Tim to resolve his problem.

It is in every video-store!

TARGET GROUPS: Depression, anxiety and adolescent groups.

COMPETENT TO MAKE…THE WRONG DECISION?

WHOSE LIFE IS IT ANYWAY? (1981)

There is a misperception among the public and even at times in the professional circles that the ability to make decisions on the part of the individual is always proportionate to his/her ending up in making the right decision.

WRONG!

Have not we ever made a wrong decision while we possess our faculties necessary for this process?

Of course, we have…

In fact, it is our wrong decision that teaches us, if we have enough wisdom to learn from our mistakes, to form a right decision relevant to future happenings.

The hospital setting is not much different than that of any other premises.

Richard Dreyfuss portrays a promising young sculptor who has an accident in the beginning of the movie, ending up as a rehab hospital quadriplegic, not being able to feel or move anything below his neck!

After six months, he asks the hospital to stop providing him with artificial support so he can die peacefully. This generates furor among the clinicians and administrators. The hospital-appointed psychiatrist finds him incompetent to make such a decision due to his morbid depression. The psychiatrist who has been designated by Richard's lawyer within the line of expert opinion however, thinks that the patient is in full command of his faculties relevant to consenting qualities.

The cross-examining attorney asks this psychiatrist whether the patient is making a right or wrong decision during the testimony. His answer is "his making a wrong decision."

This answer is even misinterpreted by the patient's attorney who utters, out of frustration, an "S" word! After all, he, like most of the people identifies competency with an ability to make "the right decision!"

The judge finally extends his conclusion in favor of the patient's wish. The administrator still wants him to stay in the hospital voluntarily and offers to assist him as long as he wants his staff to provide care. Richard's character accepts this arrangement. The last scene of the movie shows his being back in his bed, visualizing one of the art pieces he produced during the time before the unfortunate accident. The classical music soundtrack enhances this final scene to bring tears to our eyes!

This clip generates debate-like quality discussions among the participants. The group members are usually divided regarding his ability to make decisions to serve his best interest concerning the matters of his well-being. However, the same 50-50 divisions are not necessarily observed while discussing his doing right vs. wrong decision. The majority of the people usually believe that he is doing either the right or the wrong thing!

This vignette is also important regarding the discussion of those physician-assisted suicides, the contemporary and controversial issue with complicated clinical, ethical and legal parameters.

TARGET GROUPS: Terminal patients and their loved ones, caregivers, media and lawyer groups.

MARRIAGE BY LOGIC

SCENES FROM THE MALL (1991)

Here is the clip with an interesting TA exemplification!

Woody Allen and Bette Midler portray a couple shopping in the mall during the Christmas Holiday. They shock each other when they voluntarily confess their affairs! After prophesizing a lot of "should not", "must not" and "have to" of the Parental selves and displaying anger, resentment and disappointment of the Child selves, the couple sit on the bench, exhausted...

They raise the question why they have been married to each other more than twenty years... Suddenly, each one starts listing to the other one's "good" sides, and two people who were ready to strangle each other a couple of minutes before, are engaged in quite a productive conversation reflective of their Adult selves. Both of them realize that they have more in common than they can even imagine. They realize what happens to some if not most marriages, i.e. slowly drifting away from each other without even realizing it, has happened to them. In the end, they decide to stay in the marriage while ready to revitalize it. It is a happy ending film but quite a realistic one, as neither of them run at each other with affectations!

This clip is quite prophylactic in its message: We need to keep our relationships healthy with regular "check-ups" before it is strayed out. A good relationship (Child to Child) may not necessarily be a healthy one (Adult to Adult). A healthy relationship is founded on logic and reasoning in the very same way these two figure out in the movie...the hard way!

RELATIONSHIP GROUPS

TELL US THE PERSON WITH WHOM

YOU DO NOT GET ALONG, AT ALL ...

... IN FACT, YOU HATE HIS/HER GUTS!

NOW, LET US KNOW SOMETHING

GOOD ABOUT THIS PERSON!

IS IT EASY FOR YOU TO TALK ABOUT

GOOD QUALITIES THE PEOPLE POSSESS?

SAM PECKINPAH AND…HUMOR THERAPY?

WILD BUNCH (1969)

"Yeah, right!" you may say…but it is true!

One of the best movie clips exemplifying the importance of humor has not necessarily been extracted from one of those Woody Allen movies but rather from Sam Peckinpah's Wild Bunch…

Bill Holden, who portrays a leader of the aged outlaws, takes the gang back to their safe haven after the bloody bank robbery and a violent shoot out. They however, find out that they are duped! The useless metals have replaced the gold in the bags! Apparently, the people have been informed about the said robbery before the gang arrived in town.

This situation immediately generates agitation, mutual accusations, resentment, sarcasm, and cynicism among the gang members. The whole incident escalates, insults fly in the air, and it even ends up with some of them pulling guns on the other ones. Suddenly, the highly charged atmosphere leads to deadly silence, as everybody realizes that the situation has gotten out of hand. and they sit down, exhausted…

Bill Holden's character, still feeling responsible for doing something to uplift the spirit of his gang, makes a joke in the middle of nowhere… Warren Oates' character laughs at that… Jamie Sanchez' character smiles… Edmund O'Brien's character giggles… Ben Johnson's character cracks up… Ernest Borgnine's character loses it… Each one adds another joke relevant to what their leader started and suddenly all the group members who were just ready to kill each other moments before, start acting like a bunch of elementary school kids having a good time at the birthday party!

Humor is very important, anytime…anywhere…

HUMOR AND PROBLEM SOLVING GROUPS

DOES HUMOR CAUSE PROBLEMS?

IS HUMOR INFECTIOUS?

IS IT ONE OF DEFENSE MECHANISMS
WE USE TO ALLEVIATE STRESS?

DISCUSS DIFFERENT HUMOR TYPES…

Appendix-A

Psychiatrist portrayals in the US produced movies

1906-2002

PSYCHIATRIST PORTRAYALS IN THE US PRODUCED MOVIES BETWEEN

1906 AND 2002

1) This is the list of those US productions depicting psychiatrists and does not include international movies, TV pictures or documentaries.

2) Some movies were co-produced by the international movie industry hence their inclusion in the list.

3) The psychiatric portrayal for each given picture is quantitative only. In other words, the psychiatrist's appearance may be limited to very brief scene.

4) The list includes the films rates of which may be General [G], Parental Guidance [PG], Parental Guidance-13 [PG-13], Restricted [R] and Adults only [X]. Therefore, the adult viewers are expected to exercise caution before sharing the movie with the minors.

5) The majority of the movies portray psychiatrists within the perspective of relevance and reliability of the list but there may be other therapists in a few such as psychologists, social workers, and educational instructors.

6) "The", "a" and "an" have been intentionally omitted to avoid confusion as some movies include these while the other ones do not

ABBOTT AND CASTELLO MEET THE INVISIBLE MAN-1951
ABNORMAL FEMALE-1969
ACE VENTURA, PET DEDECTIVE-1994
ADULTERY-1987
ADVENTURES OF LUCKY PIERRE-1963
ADVENTURES OF RUSTY-1945
ADVENTURES OF THE ROAD RUNNER-1962
AFTER THE BALL WAS OVER-1969
AFTER THE THIN MAN-1936
AGONY OF LOVE-1966
AIRPLANE II-1983
ALICE-1990
ALICE SWEET ALICE-1977
ALL THE WRONG PLACES-2000
ALLEY TRAMP-1968
ALLIGATOR EYES-1990
ALLIGATOR PEOPLE-1959
ALOHA OE-1912
ALONE IN THE DARK-1982
ALTAR OF LUST-1971
AMERICAN MATCHMAKER-1940
AMERICAN PERFEKT-1997
AMOS AND ANDREW-1993
AMITYVILLE-1992
ANALYZE THIS-1999
ANALYZE THAT-2002
ANATOMY OF MURDER-1959
ANTZ-1998
ANGEL DUSTED-1981
ANGEL HEART-1987
ANGEL ON MY SHOULDER-1946
ANIMAL IMPULSE-1985
ANNIE HALL-1977
ANOTHER TIME, ANOTHER PLACE-1958
ANOTHER WOMAN-1988
APPLEBY SENSATION-1992
ARTICLE 99-1992
ARRANGEMENT-1969
ARSENIC AND OLD LACE-1944
ARTISTS AND BRAIN SPECIALISTS-1912
AS GOOD AS IT GETS-1997
ASYLUM OF SATAN-1972
ATTACK OF THE FIFTY FEET WOMAN-1958
ATTACK OF THE FIFTY FEET WOMAN-1993
AUTOMATIC-2001
AUTUMN LEAVES-1956

AVENGING DISCO GODFATHER-1977
AWAKENINGS-1990
BABY DOLL-1956
BABY GENUISES-1999
BABYLON PINK III-1988
BACHELOR AND THE BOBY SOXER-1947
BACKDRAFT-1991
BAD BOYS-1983
BAD DREAMS-1988
BAD GIRLS IN THE MOVIES-1986
BANG, BANG, YOU'VE GOT IT-1975
BARBARA'S PSYCHIATRIST-1970
BARBIE'S PHANTASIES-1974
BASEMENT AND THE KITCHEN-1999
BASIC INSTINCT-1992
BEAUTIFUL MIND-2001
BEDTIME STORY-1964
BEHIND LOCKED DOORS-1948
BELL JAR-1979
BELL, BARE AND BEAUTIFUL-1963
BENNY AND JOON-1993
BEST IN SHOW-2000
BEWITCHED-1945
BEYOND THERAPY-1987
BI-BI LOVE-1985
BIG CHILL-1984
BIG JIM MCLAIN-1952
BILL & TED'S EXCELLENT ADVENTURE-1989
BIONCA ON FIRE-1988
BIRCH INTERVAL-1976
BIRD-1988
BIRDY-1985
BITTERSWEET LOVE-1976
BLACK BORDERED LETTER-1911
BLACK CAT-1934
BLACK MOON-1934
BLACK WITH SUGAR-1989
BLACKTHORN ROSE-1998
BLAZE-1989
BLISS-1997
BLINDFOLD-1966
BLONDE ON THE RUN-1986
BLONDIE KNOWS BEST-1946
BLOOD FRENZY-1987
BLOOD BROTHERS-1978
BLOODY WEDNESDAY-1987

BLUE SKY-1994
BLUEBEARD'S EIGHTH WIFE-1938
BLUME IN LOVE-1973
BOB & CAROL & TED & ALICE-1969
BODY ARTS-1991
BODY PUZZLE-1994
BODILY HARM-1995
BODY OF INFLUENCE-1993
BODY SNATCHERS-1994
BOOGEY MAN-1980
BOOGEYMAN-1982
BOOGEYMAN III-1994
BORIS & NATASHA-1992
BOTTLE ROCKET-1996
BOY WHO CRIED BITCH-1991
BOY WHO CRIED WEREWOLF-1973
BOY WITH THE GREEN HAIR-1948
BRAINSTORM-1965
BRAINSUCKER-1988
BRASS BOTTLE-1963
BREAKING POINT-1989
BRIDAL SUITE-1939
BRIDE AND THE BEAST-1958
BRIGHT VICTORY-1951
BRILLIANT DISGUISE-1994
BRINGING UP BABY-1938
BRONCO BILLY-1980
BROOD-1979
BROTHERS-2001
BULLDOG DRUMMOND-1929
BULLETPROOF HEART-1994
BULLETS OVER BROADWAY-1994
BUTCHER BOY-1997
BUTCHER'S WIFE-1991
BUTTERFIELD 8-1960
BYE BYE LOVE-1995
CABINET OF CALIGARI-1962
CAINE MUTINY-1954
CALLING ALL DOCTORS-1937
CALLING DR. PORKY-1940
CAPTAIN NEWMAN, MD-1964
CAREFREE-1938
CARETAKERS-1963
CARNIVAL OF SOULS-1962
CASE OF BECKY-1915
CASE OF BECKY-1921

CASE OF THE HOWLING DOG-1934
CAT PEOPLE-1942
CAUGHT-1949
CECIL BE DEMENTED-2000
CELEBRITY-1998
CHAFED ELBOWS-1967
CHAIR-1988
CHAMBER-1996
CHAMELEON-1989
CHAMELEON-1995
CHAMELEON STREET-1991
CHAPPAQUA-1967
CHARLEY'S GIRLS-1988
CHARLIE CHAN IN HONOLULU-1939
CHARLY-1968
CHARMED AGAIN-1989
CHATTAHOOCHEE-1989
CHATTERBOX!-1977
CHEAPER TO KEEP HER-1981
CHECKERED COAT-1948
CHECKING OUT-1989
CHILD'S PLAY-1988
CHILDREN'S GAMES-1969
CHOOSE ME-1984
CIAO! MANHATTAN-1972
CLARA'S HEART-1988
CLIMAX-1954
COAST TO COAST-1980
COBWEB-1955
COLD FEET-1984
COMA-1978
COMBAT SHOCK-1984
COME FILL THE CUP-1951
COME PLAY WITH ME-1968
COMING APART-1969
COMMITTED-1983
COMMITTED-2000
COMMUNION-1989
CONFESSION-1999
CONSPIRACY THEORY-1997
COUCH-1961
COUCH IN NEW YORK-1995
COUCH TRIP-1988
CRAFT-1996
CRAZY PEOPLE-1990
CRAZY QUILT-1966

CRAZY WORLD OF JULIUS VROODER-1974
CRIME DOCTOR, SIX MOVIES BETWEEN 1943 AND 1949
CRIMINAL HYPNOTIST-1909
CRIMINAL PASSION-1994
CRITIC'S CHOICE-1963
CRITICAL CONDITION-1987
CRITICAL POSITIONS-1987
CROOKED WAY-1949
CROWN JEWEL OF INDONESIA-1999
CRUEL INTENTIONS-1999
CUB REPORTER-1909
CURFEW-1989
CURSE-1999
CURVE-1998
CURSE OF THE ALFA STONE-1985
DADDY'S GONE A HUNTING-1969
DAFFY RENTS-1966
DANGEROUS ATTENTION-1999
DANGEROUS GAME-1941
DANGEROUSLY THEY LIVE-1942
DANIEL-1983
DARK ASYLUM-2001
DARK CITY-1998
DARK GODDESS-1994
DARK MIRROR-1946
DARK PAST-1948
DARK ROMANCES, VOLUME I & II-1990
DAUGHTERS OF SATAN-1972
DAVID AND LISA-1962
DAY OF THE NIGHTMARE-1965
DEAD AGAIN-1991
DEAD BY MONDAY-2000
DEAD CERTAIN-1990
DEAD MAN OUT-1989
DEAD-BANG-1989
DEAD OF WINTER-1987
DEAD PIT-1989
DEAD POOL-1988
DEAD SILENT-1999
DEAD SLEEP-1990
DEAR BRIGITTE-1965
DEATH BECOMES HER-1992
DEATH DRUG-1978
DEATH IN THE AIR-1937
DEBAUCHERS-1972
DECEIVER-1998
DECEPTIONS TWO-1995

DECONSTRUCTING HARRY-1997
DEEP THROAT-1972
DEEP THROAT II-1987
DEAR HUNTER-1978
DEFIANCE-1974
DEMENTIA 13-1963
DEMON SEED-1977
DEMONSOUL-1994
DESIRE-1936
DESIRE ME-1947
DESPERATE CHARACTERS-1971
DESPERATE LIVING-1977
DESPERATE MOVES-1986
DEDECTIVE-1968
DEVIL'S OWN-1966
DIAL 1119-1950
DIARY OF A MAD HOUSEWIFE-1970
DIARY OF A SWINGER-1967
DIRTY MOVIES-1989
DIRTY LAUNDRY-1998
DIRTY ROTTEN SCOUNDRELS-1988
DISHONORED LADY-1947
DISORDERLY ORDERLY-1964
DISTURBED-1990
DISTURBING BEHAVIOR-1998
DIVORCE: A CONTEMPORARY WESTERN-1998
DOCTOR DESIRE-1984
DOCTOR X-1932
DOCTORS' WIVES-1971
DOG PARK-1998
DON'T GIVE UP THE SHIP-1959
DON'T LOOK IN THE BASEMENT-1973
DON'T SAY A WORD-2002
DON JUAN DE MARCO-1995
DOOMED LOVE-1984
DOPPELGANGER-1993
DOUBLE INITIATION-1970
DOWN AND OUT IN BEVERLY HILLS-1986
DR. CALIGARI-1989
DR. DIPPY'S SANITARIUM-1906
DR.DOLITTLE-1998
DR. DRACULA-1981
DR. GIGGLES-1992
DR. JEKYLL AND MS. HIDE-1995
DR. PARADISE-1988
DR. SEX-1964

DR. T. & THE WOMEN-2000
DRACULA-1931
DRACULA-1979
DRACULA: DEAD AND LOVING IT-1995
DRACULA SUCKS-1979
DRACULA'S DAUGHTER-1936
DRAGONFLY-1976
DREAM LOVER-1986
DREAM NO EVIL-1971
DREAM TEAM-1989
DREAMANIAC-1987
DREAMS IN THE FORBIDDEN ZONE I-1988
DREAMS OF MISTY-1985
DREAMS OF NATASHA-1985
DRESSED TO KILL-1980
DRIVE, HE SAID-1971
DRUG TAKING AND THE ARTS-1994
EDEN IS BURNING-1989
EDUCATION AND SONNY CARSON-1974
EDWARD SCISSORHANDS-1990
"11"-1980
ELI ELI-1940
EMBERS-1916
EMPTY MIRROR/FREUD-1999
END-1978
END OF INNOCENCE-1990
END OF THE ROAD-1970
ENDLESS LOVE-1981
ENTITY-1982
EPITAPH-1987
EQUINOX-1970
EROTIC ADVENTURES OF CASANOVA-1979
EVENING STAR-1996
EVERY MAN'S FANCY-1988
EVERYONE SAYS I LOVE YOU-1996
EVERYTHING IS DUCKY-1961
EX-1997
EXIT IN RED-1996
EXORCIST-1973
EXORCISTII-1977
EXORCIST III-1990
EXPERIMENT PERILOUS-1944
EXPERT-1994
EYE OF THE BEHOLDER-1992
EYE ON THE SPARROW-1987
FANNY-1995

FAR OUT MAN-1990
FAUST-1964
FEAR STRIKES OUT-1957
FEARLESS-1993
FEEDBACK-1963
FEMALE PERVERSIONS-1996
FIFTH AVENUE GIRL-1939
FIFTH FLOOR-1980
FILTHY RICH-1970
FINAL-2001
FINAL ANALYSIS-1992
FINAL APPROACH-1991
FINE MADNESS-1966
FINGERS-1978
FINGERS AT THE WINDOW-1942
FIRE SALE-1977
FIRST WIVES CLUB-1996
FIVE STEPS TO DANGER-1957
FIXED BY GEORGE-1920
FLAME WITHIN-1935
FLESHBURN-1984
FLOODING-2000
FLY BY NIGHT-1942
FOILED-2000
FOOL AND THE DANCER-1915
FOOLS-1970
FORCE-1994
FOREVER DARLING-1956
FOREVER JUNG-1995
FOURTEEN HOURS-1951
FRANCES-1982
FRANKENSTEIN GENERAL HOSPITAL-1988
FREAK-1999
FREDDY GOT FINGERED-2001
FRESH KILL-1994
FREUD-1962
FREUD-1984
FRIDAY THE 13TH, PART V-1985
FRIDAY THE 13TH, PART VII-1988
FRIGHT NIGHT, PART 2-1988
FROM BEYOND-1986
FROM NOON TILL THREE-1976
FROM NURSE TO WORSE-1940
FROM THE TERRACE-1960
FRONT PAGE-1931
FRONT PAGE-1974

FULL MOON HIGH-1982
FUN-1994
FURY-1978
FUTURE SHOCK-1993
GAMES-1967
GARMENTS OF TRUTH-1921
GATHERING OF EVIL-1969
GAY DECEIVERS-1969
GAY INTRUDERS-1948
GENERAL'S DAUGHTER-1999
GET A JOB-1998
GET THAT GIRL-1932
GETTING AWAY WITH MURDER-1996
GINGERBREAD MAN-1998
GINGER'S SEX ASYLUM-1985
GIRL, INTERRUPTED-1999
GLEN OR GLENDA-1953
GNOME-MOBILE-1967
GODDESS-1915
GOING BERSERK-1983
GOING UNDER-1990
GOLD CURE-1919
GOLDENGIRL-1979
GOOD ENOUGH TO EAT-1988
GOOD WILL HUNTING-1997
GOODNIGHT, SWEET MARILYN-1989
GORILLA MAN-1942
GRACE QUIGLEY-1984
GREETINGS-1968
GREY ZONE-1997
GROSSE POINT BLANK-1997
GROUNDHOG DAY-1993
GROUP-1966
GUEST IN THE HOUSE-1944
GUNSHY-2000

HANGOVER SQUARE-1944
HANNIBAL-2001
HAPPINESS-1998
HAPPINESS CAGE-1972
HARD SOAP, HARD SOAP-1977
HARRIETT THE SPY-1996
HAROLD AND MAUDE-1971
HARVEY-1950
HARVEY MIDDLEMAN, FIREMAN-1965
HAUNTED HONEYMOON-1986
HAUNTING FEAR-1990
HEAVEN-1998
HEARSE-1980
HEDONISTIC PLEASURES-1969
HELLHOLE-1985
HENRY'S NIGHT IN-1969
HER FINAL RECKONING-1918
HERO AND THE TERROR-1988
HEROES-1977
HIGH ANXIETY-1977
HIGH RISE-1972
HIGH WALL-1947
HILLS HAVE EYES II-1985
HIS GIRL FRIDAY-1940
HITLER TAPES-1994
HOLD THAT BABY!-1949
HOLD THAT BLONDE-1945
HOLIDAY FOR LOVERS-1959
HOLLOW TRIUMPH-1948
HOME OF THE BRAVE-1949
HONOLULU-1939
HORROR SHOW-1989
HOSPITAL-1971
HOT BLOODED WOMAN-1965
HOT SHOTS-1991
HOUSE OF CARDS-1968
HOUSE OF CARDS-1993
HOUSE OF DARKNESS-1913
HOUSE OF GAMES-1987
HOUSE OF SECRETS-1936
HAUSE ON HAUNTED HILL-1959
HOUSE ON HAUNTED HILL-1999
HOWLIN-1981
HUDSUCKER PROXY-1994
HUMAN EXPERIMENTS-1980
HUSBANDS AND WIVES-1992

I AM THE CHEESE-1983
I LOVE MY WIFE-1970
I LOVE YOU...DON'T TOUCH ME!-1998
I LOVE YOU MADLY-1935
I NEVER PROMISED YOU A ROSE GARDEN-1977
I SHOT ANDY WARHOL-1996
I WANT YOU-1974
I WAS A TEENAGE WEREWOLF-1957
I AM DANCING AS FAST AS I CAN-1982
I'M LOSING YOU-1998
ICE CREAM MAN-1995
ICE HOUSE-1969
IMAGINARY LOVERS-1986
IMMORAL MR.TEAS-1959
IMP-1919
IMPOSSIBLE YEARS-1968
IMPULSE-1990
IN CROWD-2000
IN DREAMS-1998
IN PERSON-1935
IN SARAH'S EYES-1976
IN THE COLD OF THE NIGHT-1989
IN THE HEAT OF PASSION-1992
IN THE MOUTH OF MADNESS-1995
INDEPENDENCE-1976
INEVITABLE GRACE-1994
INFRASEXUM-1968
INKWELL-1994
INNER SANCTUM II-1994
INNOCENT OBSESSION-1989
INSIDE OUT-1992
INSIDE MONKEY-ZETTERLAND-1992
INSPIRATION-1982
INSTANT KARMA-1991
INSTINCT-1999
INTERNS-1962
INTIMATE DECEPTION-1996
INVADERS FROM MARS-1953
INVASION OF THE BODY SNATCHERS-1956
INVASION OF THE BODY SNATCHERS-1978
INVISIBLE GHOST-1941
ISLAND, ALICIA-1998
IT'S ABOUT TIME-1992
IT'S IN THE BAG-1945
IT'S MY TURN-1980
IVORY SNUFFBOX-1915

I'VE LIVED BEFORE-1956
JADE-1995
JAGGED EDGE-1985
JAIL BUSTERS-1955
JAILBIRD ROCK-1985
JANE DOE-1983
JOANNA STORM ON FIRE-1986
JOHNNY EAGER-1942
JUGGLER-1953
JUDGMENT DAY: THE ELLIE NESTER STORY-1999
JULIA-1977
JUNGLE GIRL-1944
KEEP MY GRAVE OPEN-1980
KID-2000
KIDS ON THE HALL: BRIAN CANDY-1996
KILLER-1994
KILLER OBSESSION-1994
KIMBERLEY-1999
KINGS ROW-1942
KISS AND TELL-1997
KLUTE-1971
KNEEL BEFORE ME!-1983
KNOCK ON WOOD-1954
K-PAX-2001
LACY AFFAIR-1983
LADY GAMBLES-1949
LADY IN A JAM-1942
LADY IN THE CAR WITH GLASSES AND A GUN-1970
LADY IN THE DARK-1944
LADY ON THE COUCH-1978
LAND OF JAZZ-1920
LAST EMBRACE-1979
LAST GENTLEMAN-1934
LAST RITES-1998
LAST SPACE VOYAGE OF WALLACE RAMSEL-1978
LATIN LOVERS-1953
LAY OF THE LAND-1997
LEAVE IT TO BEAVER-1997
LEGACY-1975
LEGACY OF BLOOD-1971
LET THERE BE LIGHT-1946
LET'S LIVE A LITTLE-1948
LETHAL WEAPON-1987
LETHAL WEAPON 2-1989
LETHAL WEAPON 3-1992
LETHAL WEAPON 4-1998

LETTING GO-1998
LIES-1984
LIFE ON THE EDGE-1988
LIFEFORCE-1985
LIFESPAN-1975
LIGHTIN' IN THE FORREST-1948
LILITH-1964
LILITH UNLEASHED-1986
LINE-1980
LINEAGE-1997
LITTLE MISS BIG-1946
LITTLE TOUGH GUYS IN SOCIETY-1938
LIVING IN A WET DREAM-1988
LIZZIE-1957
LOADED WEAPON I-1993
LOCAL HERO-1983
LOCKET-1946
LONELY LADY-1983
LONELY NIGHT-1954
LONELY SEX-1959
LONG GOODBYE-1973
LOST ANGELS-1989
LOST HOUSE-1915
LOST, LONELY AND VICIOUS-1958
LOST SOULS-2000
LOU, PAT AND JOE D.-1988
LOVE AT FIRST BITE-1979
LOVE BUS-1976
LOVE CAPTIVE-1934
LOVE COUCH-1977
LOVE CRAZY-1941
LOVE DOCTOR-1929
LOVE IN THE STRANGE PLACES-1972
LOVE ME...PLEASE-1969
LOVESICK-1983
LOVE STORY-1979
LOVE STREAMS-1984
LOVE SWEDISH STYLE-1972
LOVE-MY WAY-1966
LOVER COME BACK-1961
LOVES OF A PSYCHIATRIST-1968
LOVING LULU-1993
LUCKY DEVIL-1925
LUNATIC ASYLUM-1925
LUNATIC AT LARGE-1927
LUNATICS IN POWER-1909

LUST AND REVENGE-1996
LUST AT FIRST BITE-1979
LUST FOR LIFE-1956
LUST INFERNO-1983
LYCANTHROPE-1997
MABEL RENSHAW-1910
MAD ABOUT YOU-1987
MAD DOCTOR-1941
MAD LOVE-1995
MADE FOR EACH OTHER-1971
MADHOUSE-1981
MADNESS OF KING GEORGE III-1994
MAGIC IN THE WATER-1995
MAGIC OF MARCIANO-2000
MAGUS-1968
MAISIE GOES TO RIO-1944
MAJOR LEAGUE II-1994
MAKE A FACE-1971
MAKE ME SWEAT-1989
MAN IN THE NET-1959
MAN IN THE TRUNK-1942
MAN ON A SWING-1974
MAN WHO CRIED WOLF-1937
MAN WHO TURNED TO STONE-1957
MAN-MADE MONSTER-1941
MANCHURIAN CANDIDATE-1962
MANHANDLED-1949
MANHUNTER-1986
MANIC-2000
MANIFESTO-1988
MARIA'S LOVERS-1985
MARRIAGE OF YOUNG STOCK BROKER-1971
MARRY ME AGAIN-1953
MARRY THE GIRL-1937
MARVIN'S ROOM-1996
MARTIANS, GO HOME-1990
MARY'S LAMB-1915
MASK-1994
MASTER HAND-1915
MATRIMONIAL BED-1930
MAUSOLEUM-1983
MAXIMUM SECURITY-1987
McHALE'S NAVY-1997
ME AND MY BROTHER-1969
MEAN SEASON-1985
MEET THE CHUMP-1941

MERCY-1999
MIAMI RHAPSODY-1995
MIDNIGHT RIDE-1990
MIDNIGHT TEASE-1994
MIDNIGHT WARNING-1932
MIDNIGHT ZONE-1986
MILLERSON CASE-1947
MILLION DOLLAR DOLLIES-1918
MILLION IN PEARLS-1914
MILLIONAIRE FOR CHRISTY-1951
MIND BLOWERS-1968
MIND LIES-1996
MINISTRY OF FEAR-1944
MIRACLE ON THE 34TH STREET-1947
MIRAGE-1965
MISSING PLACES-1991
MODERN MARRIAGE-1950
MOMENT TO MOMENT-1966
MONDO TRASHO-1970
MONIQUE-1985
MONKEY BONE-2001
MONKEY BUSINESSMEN-1948
MONKEY ON MY BACK-1957
MOON IN SCORPIO-1988
MORE THAN SISTERS-1979
MOTHER DIDN'T TELL ME-1950
MOTHER GOOSE A GO-GO-1966
MOTHER'S BOYS-1993
MOVE-1970
MOVE OVER DARLING-1963
MOVIE STAR, AMERICAN STYLE or LSD, I HATE YOU-1966
MOVIES, MONEY, MURDER-1996
MR. BUGHOUSE IS CURED-1912
MR. BUMPTIOUS, DEDECTIVE-1911
MR. BUTT-IN-1906
MR. DEEDS GO TO TOWN-1936
MR. FROST-1990
MR. JEALOUSY-1997
MR. JONES-1993
MR. PEABODY AND THE MERMAID-1948
MRS. PARKER AND THE VICIOUS CIRCLE-1994
MOTHER-1994
MUGGER-1957
MURDER AT THE GLEN ATHOL-1936
MURDER, MY SWEET-1944
MUTT AND JEFF AND ESCAPED LUNATIC-1911

MY FAVORITE WIFE-1940
MY LIFE'S IN TURNAROUND-1993
MY LITTLE GIRL-1986
MY NEXT FUNERAL-2000
MY TWO LOVES-1986
MY WORLD DIES SCREAMING-1958
MYSTERIOUS STRANGER-1915
MYSTERY MAN-1999
MYSTERY STREET-1950
MYTH OF FINGERPRINTS-1997
NAKED FACE-1984
NAKED FRAILTIES-1998
NAKED VENGEANCE-1986
NATURAL ENEMIES-1979
NET-1995
NEVER TALK TO STRANGERS-1995
NEW INTERNS-1964
NEW YEAR'S DAY-1989
NEW YORK STORIES-1989
NICE GIRLS DON'T EXPLODE-1987
NIGHT CALL NURSES-1974
NIGHT MONSTER-1942
NIGHT OF BLOODY HORROR-1969
NIGHT EYES 4-1995
NIGHT PATROL-1985
NIGHT PORTER-1974
NIGHT RUNNER-1957
NIGHT STALKER-1987
NIGHT TRAIN TO TERROR-1985
NIGHT VISITOR-1970
NIGHT WARS-1988
NIGHT WITHOUT SLEEP-1952
NIGHTBREED-1990
NIGHTLIFE-1983
NIGHTMARE-1981
NIGHTMARE AT SHADOW WOODS-1984
NIGHTMARE ON ELM STREET-1984
NIGHTMARE ON ELM STREET 3-1987
NIGHTMARE ON ELM STREET 5-1989
NINE MONTHS-1995
1999-1998
91ST DAY-1964
NINTH CONFIGURATION-1980
NO ONE MAN-1932
NO RETURN ADDRESS-1961
NO TIME FOR SARGEANTS-1958

NOBODY'S PERFEKT-1981
NOMADS-1986
NOOSE HANGS HIGH-1949
NORMA-1970
NOW, VOYAGER-1942
NUN'S STORY-1958
NURSE SHERRI-1977
NUTTY PROFESSOR II: THE KLUMPS-2000
NUTS-1987
OCCHIO PINOCCHIO-1994
OCCULT PLEASURES-1983
ODYSSEY-1977
OH, GOD! BOOK II-1980
OLD BOYFRIENDS-1979
OLIVER'S STORY-1978
OMEN-1976
ON A CLEAR DAY YOU CAN SEE FOREVER-1970
ON HER BED OF ROSES-1966
ON THE YARD-1978
ONCE UPON A TEMPTRESS-1988
ONCE YOU KISS A STRANGER-1969
ONE FINE DAY-1996
ONE FLEW OVER THE CUCKOO'S NEST-1975
ONE HYSTERICAL NIGHT-1929
ONE NIGHT AT MCCOOL'S-2001
ONE PAGE OF LOVE-1983
ONLY IN MY DREAMS-1970
OPPOSITE SEX-1956
ORDINARY PEOPLE-1980
OTHER VOICES-2000
OUT OF BLUE-1980
OUT ON A LIMB-1992
OVERBOARD-1987
PANIC-2000
PAPERTRAIL-1997
PARENTS-1989
PARIS HOLIDAY-1958
PARK AVENUE LOGGER-1937
PARANOIA-1998
PAROLE!-1936
PASSION OF MIND-2000
PASSION STREET, USA-1964
PATCH ADAMS-1998
PEEPING TOM-1986
PEEPHOLE-1992
PENELOPE-1966

PEOPLE NEXT DOOR-1970
PERFECT BRAT-1989
PERILS OF P.K.-1986
PHANTASMAGORIA-1996
PHANTOM-1931
PHFFFT!-1954
PINOCCHIO'S REVENGE-1996
PLACE BEYOND SHAME-1979
PLASTERED IN PARIS-1928
PLAYGROUND-1965
PLEASE DON'T TOUCH ME-1959
PLEASE, PLEASE ME-1976
PLEDGE-2001
POLTERGEIST III-1988
POLYESTER-1982
POOR ALBERT AND LITTLE ANNY-1972
POSSESSED-1947
POSSESSION OF JOEL DELANEY-1972
PRESCRIPTION: MURDER-1968
PRESSURE POINT-1962
PRETTY PEACHES III (THE QUEST)-1982
PRIMAL FEAR-1996
PRINCE OF TIDES-1991
PRISON BABIES-1976
PRISON GIRLS-1973
PRISONER OF THE SECOND AVENUE-1975
PRIVATE EYES-1953
PRIVATE WORLDS-1935
PRIVATE'S AFFAIR-1959
PROBLEM CHILD-1990
PROGENY-1998
PROMISE-1979
PSYCHIATRIST-1971
PSYCHIATRIST-1978
PSYCHIC KILLER-1975
PSYCHO-1960
PSYCHO II-1983
PSYCHO III-1986
PSYCHO-1998
PSYCHO LOVER-1970
PSYCHOTRONIC MAN-1980
PUERTO RICAN MAMBO-1993
PUSSY CAT, PUSSY CAT, I LOVE YOU-1970
PUTTING ONE OVER-1919
PUZZLE OF A DOWNFALL CHILD-1970
QUICKSAND-2001

QUIET ONE-1949
QUILLS-2000
QUIZ SHOW-1994
RAGE IN HEAVEN-1941
REGINA'S SECRET-1969
RAIN MAN-1988
RAINY DAY FRIENDS-1989
RAMPAGE-1987
RAMPAGE-1992
RANDOM HARVEST-1942
RATS-2001
REACHING OUT-1983
REAL BLONDE-1998
REASONABLE MAN-1999
REFLECTIONS IN A GOLDEN EYE-1967
REFORMITORY-1938
RELENTLESS IV-1994
REQUIEM FOR A DREAM-2000
REST IN PIECES-1987
RESTORATION-1995
RETRIBUTION-1987
RETURN OF COUNT YORGA-1971
RETURN OF THE WHISTLER-1948
RETURN TO OZ-1985
REVENGE-1986
REVENGE OF THE DEAD-1785
REVENGE OF THE RED BARON-1994
RICH KIDS-1979
RIFT-1993
RIOT IN A JUVENILE PRISON-1959
RIVALS-1972
RIVER RED-1998
ROAD SHOW-1941
ROCK AND ROLL FRANKENSTEIN-1999
ROGUE'S GALLERY-1967
RORSCHACH-1993
ROSIE-1967
ROUND MIDNIGHT-1986
RUSSIA HOUSE-1990
SAD SACK-1957
SAFE-1995
SAFE SEX-1999
SANDRA, THE MAKING OF A WOMAN-1970
SANTA CLAUSE-1994
SAPPHO DARLING-1969
SAPS AT SEA-1940

SAVE ME-1993
SAVING SILVERMAN-2000
SCARED STIFF-1987
SCARED TO DEATH-1947
SCARF-1951
SCENES FROM THE MALL-1990
SCHIZOID-1980
SCISSORS-1991
SCOUNDRELS-1983
SCOUT-1994
SCREAM OF THE BUTTEFLY-1965
SCREAM YOUR HEAD OFF-1985
SCREAMING MIMI-1958
SEASON OF THE WITCH-1972
SEAVIEW NIGHTS-1994
SECOND SERVE-1986
SECOND WOMAN-1951
SECRET FURY-1950
SECRET HEART-1946
SECRET LIFE OF WALTER MITTY-1947
SECRET ROOM-1915
SECRETS OF A WILLING WIFE-1980
SEE YOU IN THE MORNING-1989
SENSUAL FIRE-1979
SERPENT AND THE RAINBOW-1988
SESSION NINE-2000
SEVEN YEAR ITCH-1955
SEVENTH VICTIM-1943
SEX AND THE SINGLE GIRL-1965
SEX ASYLUM II-1986
SEX ASYLUM III-1988
SEX SYMBOL-1974
SEXAHOLIC-1988
SEXSCAPE-1987
SEXUAL ODYSSEY-1985
SHADES OF GRAY-1948
SHADOW-1994
SHADOW IN THE SKY-1951
SHADOW ON THE WALL-1950
SHADOWS IN THE NIGHT-1944
SHAGGY DOG-1959
SHE DANCES ALONE-1981
SHE WOULDN'T SAY YES-1945
SHE'S OUT OF CONTROL-1989
SHE'S SO LOVELY-1997
SHE-MALE SANITARIUM-1988

SHINING VICTORY-1941
SHOCK-1946
SHOCK CORRIDOR-1963
SHOCK TREATMENT-1964
SHORT TIME-1990
SHRIKE-1955
SIGNPOST TO MURDER-1969
SILENCE OF THE HAMS-1993
SILENCE OF THE LAMBS-1991
SILENT FALL-1994
SILENT MADNESS-1984
SILENT NIGHT, BLOODY NIGHT-1983
SILENT NIGHT, DEADLY NIGHT II-1987
SILENT NIGHT, DEADLY NIGHT III-1989
SILENT RAGE-1982
SINCE YOU WENT AWAY-1944
SINTHIA: THE DEVIL'S DOLL-1968
SIX FACES OF SAMANTHA-1984
SIXTH DAY-2000
SKULL AND THE CROWN-1914
SLEEP, MY LOVE-1948
SLEEPY HEAD-2000
SLENDER THREAT-1965
SMALL CIRCLE OF FRIENDS-1980
SMASH UP: THE STORY OF A WOMAN-1947
SMASHING THE SPY RING-1939
SMILE-1974
SMORGASBORD-1983
SNAKE EYES II-1987
SNAKE PIT-1948
SNIDE AND PREJUDICE-1997
SNIPER-1952
SNOW IN SUMMER-1966
SO DARK THE NIGHT-1946
SO YOUNG, SO BAD-1950
SOCIAL PIRATES-1916
SOCIETY-1989
SOME KIND OF HERO-1982
SOME KIND OF NUT-1969
SOMETHING TO DO-1919
SOMETIME SWEET SUSAN-1974
SOMEWHERE IN THE NIGHT-1946
SONG OF BERNADETTE-1943
SORDID LIVES-2000
SORORITY HOUSE MASSACRE-1986
SORROWFUL JONES-1949

SOUTH PARK-1997
SPACE JAM-1996
SPANNER COP-1994
SPANKING THE MONKEY-1994
SPEAK OF THE DEVIL-1991
SPECTER OF EDGAR ALLEN POE-1973
SPELL OF THE HYPNOTIST-1956
SPELLBOUND-1945
SPIRIT IS WILLING-1967
SPLENDOR IN THE GRASS-1961
SPOOK BUSTERS-1946
SQUEEZE-1997
ST. IVES-1976
STAIRWAY TO LIGHT-1945
STALKED-1994
STARDUST MEMORIES-1980
START THE REVOLUTION WITHOUT ME-1970
STARTING OVER-1979
STEEL JUNGLE-1956
STEPFATHER-1986
STEPFATHER II-1989
STEPMONSTER-1993
STEPFORD WIVES-1974
STILL OF THE NIGHT-1982
STIR-1997
STONE KILLER-1973
STONEWALL-1995
STORY OF US-1999
STRAIT JACKET-1964
STRANGE CASE OF MARY PAGE-1916
STRANGE COMPULSION-1964
STRANGE ILLUSION-1945
STRANGE RAMPAGE-1967
STRANGER-1987
STRANGER BY NIGHT-1994
STRANGER IN MY BED-1987
STRANGER'S RETURN-1933
STRANGERS WHEN WE MATE-1975
STRANGLER-1964
STUCKEY'S LAST STAND-1980
STUDENT BODIES-1981
STUDENT NURSES-1970
SUBURBIA CONFIDENTIAL-1966
SUDDENLY, LAST SUMMER-1959
SURF NAZIS MUST DIE-1987
SURVIVING THE GAME-1994

SWEET SUSAN SLEPT HERE-1954
SUTURE-1994
SWEAT-1986
SWEET DREAMS SUZAN-1980
SWEET RIDE-1968
SWINGIN' ALONG-1962
SWOON-1992
SYBIL-1977
SYLVIA-1976
SYLVIA'S GIRLS-1965
TABOO, AMERICAN STYLE, PARTS 1, 2 AND 4-1985
TABOO IV: THE YOUNGER GENERATION-1985
TAIJA RAE-1987
TAKE IT BIG-1944
TAKE THE MONEY AND RUN-1969
TAKIN' IT OFF-1985
TAKING OFF-1971
TAMMY TELL ME TRUE-1961
TASTE OF CATNIP-1966
TEAHOUSE OF THE AUGUST MOON-1956
TEENAGE DEVIATE-1976
TEENIE TULIP-1970
10-1979
TENDER IS THE NIGHT-1961
TERROR FIRMER-1999
TERROR TRACK-2000
TERESA-1951
TERMINAL MAN-1974
TERMINATOR 2-1991
THANK YOUR LUCKY STARS-1943
THAT CERTAIN FEELING-1956
THAT TOUCH OF MINK-1962
THAT'S MY BOY-1951
THEM!-1954
THERE GOES THE GROOM-1937
THERE GOES THE NEIGHBORHOOD-1992
THERE IS NO 13-1974
SOMETHING ABOUT MARY-1998
THEY ALL COME OUT-1939
THEY MIGHT BE GIANTS-1971
THEY STILL CALL ME BRUCE-1987
THIRD OF A MAN-1962
13 HOURS BY AIR-1936
13 RUE MADELEINE-1946

36 HOURS-1964
36 HOURS TO KILL-1936
THIS FILM IS ALL ABOUT-1986
THIS WON'T HURT A BIT-1993
THOMAS CROWN AFFAIR-1999
THREE FACES OF EVE-1957
THREE KIDS AND A QUEEN-1935
THREE LOVES HAS NANCY-1938
THREE NUTS IN A SEARCH OF A BOLT-1964
THREE ON A COUCH-1966
THREE SAPPY PEOPLE-1939
THREESOME-1969
THRILL OF IT ALL-1963
TICKET TO PARADISE-1936
TIGHTROPE-1984
TIME BOMB-1992
TIME OF THEIR LIVES-1946
TIME TO KILL-1996
TIMES SQUARE-1980
TIME'S UP-2000
T.N.T. (THE NAKED TRUTH)-1924
TO BE FREE-1972
TOMORROW AND TOMORROW-1932
TORPEDO ALLEY-1952
TOUCHED-1983
TOXIC AFFAIR-1993
TOXIC AVENGER, PART II-1989
TRAIL OF THE PINK PANTHER-1983
TRANCERS II-1991
TRANSYLVANIA 6-5000-1986
TRAUMA-1993
TRAP DOOR-1980
TRIAL AND ERROR-1997
TRICK OR TREATS-1982
TRICKS OF THE TRADE-1968
TROUBLE DAWN BELOW-1970
TROUBLEMAKER-1964
TRUTH OR DARE: A CRITICAL MADNESS-1986
TURMOIL-1916
TURN OF THE SCREW-1992
TURNING THE TABLES-1919
12 MONKEYS-1995
TWELVE STEPS TO DEATH-1995
23 HOURS-2000
TWISTED SISTERS-1988
TWO GIRLS FOR A MADMAN-1968

TWO LITTLE BEARS-1961
UNDERGROUND-1995
UNDERTAKINGS-1995
UNEARTHLY-1957
UNIFORM BEHAVIOR-1989
USED PEOPLE-1992
VALLEY OF THE ZOMBIES-1946
VAMPIRE'S KISS-1988
VANDERHOFF AFFAIR-1915
VERTIGO-1958
VICTIM OF HEREDITY-1915
VIEWER DISCRETION INVOLVED-1998
VILLAGE SLEUTH-1920
VIOLATED-1953
VIRGIN AND HER LOVER-1980
VIRGIN SUICIDES-1999
VIRGINIA-1983
VISIT-2000
VOLCANO-1976
VOYAGE TO THE BOTTOM OF THE SEA-1961
WAGER-1916
WANTED II-1999
WAR OF THE EGGS-1971
WATCHER-2000
WEB OF DECEPTION-1994
WEREWOLF OF WASHINGTON-1973
WES CRAVEN'S NEW NIGHTMARE-1994
WHAT A WAY TO GO-1964
WHAT ABOUT BOB?-1991
WHAT LIES BENEATH-2000
WHAT'S NEW PUSSY CAT?-1961
WHAT'S ON YOUR MIND?-1948
WHEN A STRANGER CALLS-1979
WHEN THE CLOUDS ROLL BY-1919
WHEN THE LIGHTS GO ON AGAIN-1944
WHERE ARE THE CHILDREN?-1985
WHERE IS MY CHILD?-1937
WHERE TRUTH LIES-1996
WHERE WERE YOU WHEN THE LIGHTS WENT OUT-1968
WHIRLPOOL-1949
WHISPERS IN THE DARK-1992
WHITE HEAT-1949
WHO IS HARRY KELLERMAN AND WHY IS HE SAYING THOSE TERRIBLE
        THINGS ABOUT ME?-1971
WHO IS JULIA?-1986
WHOSE LIFE IS IT ANYWAY?-1981

WICKED GAMES-1994
WILD IN THE COUNTRY-1961
WILD SCENE-1970
WILLIE & PHIL-1980
WILLY WONKA AND THE CHOCOLATE FACTORY-1971
WISHFUL THINKING-1990
WITCHFIRE-1985
WITHOUT WARNING-1952
WITNESS TO MURDER-1954
WOMAN IN WHITE-1912
WOMAN IN WHITE-1917
WOMAN IN WHITE-1948
WOMAN TIMES SEVEN-1967
WOMAN'S TORMENT-1978
WOMAN'S TOUCH-1988
WOMAN'S URGE-1965
WOMAN WHO LOVED MEN-1984
WORLD ACCORDING TO GINGER-1985
WORTH WINNING-1989
WOULD BE SHRINER-1912
WRONG GUYS-1988
WRONG MAN-1956
YELLOW CAB MAN-1950
YOUNG RAJAH-1922
YOUNG DR. KILDARE-1938
ZELIG-1983
Z.P.G. (ZERO POPULATION GROWTH)-1972
ZOTZ-1962

THE US PRODUCTIONS IN WHICH THE MENTAL HEALTH PROVIDERS ARE DEPICTED AS "ANALYST."

BOOMERANG-1925
CHILDREN OF LONELINESS-1937
DERANGED-1987
DR. MABUSE, THE GAMBLER-1922
DUET FOR ONE-1986
FLORENTINEDAGGER-1935
FRANCIS GOES TO THE RACES-1952
FREE LOVE-1930
HANNAH AND HER SISTERS-1986
HOME FREE ALL-1983
HUNK-1987
I, THE JURY-1953
LOVESICK-1983
MAN WHO LOVED WOMEN-1983
MANHATTAN SHAKEDOWN-1939
MANY HAPPY RETURNS-1934
MR. SKEFFINGTON-1944
NESTING-1981
NOT SINCE CASANOVA-1988
O MEN, O WOMEN-1957
OUT ON A LIMB-1992
PRESIDENT'S ANALYST-1967
REUNION IN VIENNA-1933
ROSELAND-1971
SECRET DIARY OF SIGMUND FREUD-1984
SKIN DEEP-1989
SOUL MAN-1986
TALK TO ME-1982
THAT'S LIFE-1986
THAT UNCERTAIN FEELING-1941
WHO'S BEEN SLEEPING IN MY BED?-1963
WHY WOULD I LIE?-1980

Appendix-B

**PSYCHIATRIST PORTRAYALS IN THE INTERNATIONAL MOVIES
PRODUCED BETWEEN 1906 AND 2002
(Extracted from The Celluloid Coach, Les Rabkin, PhD)**

ABBREVIATIONS

ARG: Argentina; AUS: Australia; AUST: Austria; BELG: Belgium; BRAZ: Brazil; BULG: Bulgaria; CAN: Canada; CEY: Ceylon; CHI: China; COL: Colombia; CU: Cuba; CZECH: Czechoslovakia; DEN: Denmark; EGY: Egypt; FIN: Finland; FR: France; GER: Germany (for both East and West Germany); GR: Greece; HK: Hong Kong; HUNG: Hungary; IND: India; INDO: Indonesia; ISR: Israel; IT: Italy; JAP: Japan; KOR: Korea (for both South and North); LIECH: Liechtenstein; MEX: Mexico; NETH: Netherlands; NOR: Norway; PHIL: Philippines; POL: Poland; PORT: Portugal; RUM: Rumania; RUS: Russia (including Tsarist, Revolutionary, and Post-*Glasnost* Russia); SP: Spain; SWED: Sweden; SWITZ: Switzerland; THAI: Thailand; UK: United Kingdom (including the productions of Great Britain, Scotland, Wales and Northern Ireland); VEN: Venezuela; YUGO: Yugoslavia (including Bosnia-Herzegovina, Croatia, Macedonia, Monte Negro, Serbia and Slovenia).

ABEL-NETH-1986
ABRACADABRA-JAP-1988
ACT OF VIOLENCE-UK-1980
ADRIAN AND THE ROMERS-GER-1988
AFFLICTED-POL-1988
AFTER DARKNESS-SWITZ/USA-1985
AGNES OF GOD-CAN-1985
ALCOHOL-IT-1980
ALIAS JOHN PRESTON-UK-1956
ALL I WANT IS YOU…AND YOU…AND YOU-UK-1974
ALMOST A MAN-IT-1966
ALOISE-FR-1975
ALVIN PURPLE-AUS-1975
AMAAYAKA CHAKRAVARTHI-IND-1983
AMERICAN GOTHIC-UK/CAN-1988
AMSTERDAMNED-NETH-1988
ANA-POR-1983
…AND NOW THE SCREAMING STARTS-UK-1973
AND THAT ON MONDAY MORNING-GER-1959
ANDREA-GER-1968
ANGRY EARTH-UK-1989
ANGUISH-NETH-1976
ANITA-GER-1973
ANNE TRISTER-CAN-1986
ANYONE CAN PLAY-IT-1967
ASSAULT-SWED-1969

ASTONISHED HEART-UK-1949
ASYLUM-UK-1972
AT GREEN COCKATOO BY NIGHT-GER-1958
ATTACK OF THE MUSHROOM PEOPLE-JAP-1963
AUTUMN CROCUS-UK-1934
AWAKENING-UK-1980
BAD TIMING: A SENSUAL OBSESSION-UK-1980
BAHURANI-IND-1983
BARBECUE THEM! -UK-1981
BARRIER-BUL-1979
BATON ROUGE-SP-1988
BEDROOM EYES-CAN-1984
BEGGAR GIRL'S WEDDING-UK-1915
BEHIND THE CATARACT-UK-1987
BELL OF HELL-FR/SP-1973
BERNADETTE-FR-1988
BERNADETTE OF LOURDES-FR/IT-1961
BETTY BLUE-FR-1986
BETWEEN WARS-AUST-1985
BEYOND REASON-AUS-1985
BIANCA-IT-1984
BIG DIG-GER/ISR/USA-1969
BLACK JACK-UK-1979
BLACK MONK-RUS/1988
BLACK PIT OF DR. M-MEX-1958
BLACK STOCKING-CZECH-1988
BLACKBIRD-UK/YUG-1988
BLISS-AUST-1985
BLISS OF MRS. BLOSSOM-UK-1968
BLOOD OF VAMPIRE-UK-1958
BLOODLINK-GER-1985
BLUEBEARD BLUEBEARD-IT-1987
BOBBIKINS-UK-1959
BRAIN MACHINE-UK-1954
BROTHER'S JEALOUSY-FR-1912
BROTHERLY LOVE-UK-1970
BRUTE-UK-1976
BUCKET OF BLOOD-UK-1934
BURNING ANGEL-FIN-1984
BURNING MEMORY-ISR-1989
CABINET OF DR. CALIGARI-GER-1919
CALL ME BWANA-UK-1963
CALLING PAUL TEMPLE-UK-1948
CAMILLE CLUDEL-FR-1988
CARNIVAL-FR-1953
CARRY ON DANCING-HK-1989

CARRY ON TEACHER-UK-1959
CARUSO PASCOSKI_OF POLISH ORIGIN-IT-1989
CAT AND THE CANARY-UK-1977
CAT GIRL-UK-1957
CAT IN THE BRAIN-IT-1989
C'EST LA VIE RROSE-GER-1977
CHAINED-GER-1924
CHALLENGE TO LIFE-MEX-1987
CHARMER-FR-1984
CHILD OF THE NIGHT-FR/IT-1978
CHINA RANCH-ISR-1988
CHINESE ROOM-MEX-1966
CLINIQUE-FR-1989
CLOCKWORK ORANGE-UK-1971
CLOSELY WATCHED TRAINS-CZECH-1966
CLOWNS OF GOD-FR-1986
COBWEB-CZECH-1986
COMEBACK-UK-1977
COMFORT AND JOY-UK-1984
CONDEMNED TO DEATH-UK-1932
CONFRONTATION-SWITZ-1975
CONSTANT HUSBAND-UK-1955
CORRIDOR OF MIRORS-UK-1948
COUNT DRACULA-GER/IT/SP/LICH-1970
CREATURE WITH THE BLUE HAND-GER-1967
CREEPING FLESH-UK-1972
CRIMES AT THE DARK HOUSE-UK-1940
CURTAINS-CZECH-1983
DAEMON-UK-1986
DANCE OF FIRE-ARG-1950
DANCING IN THE DARK-CAN-1986
DANGEROUS KISSES-DEN-1972
DARK PLACES-UK-1973
DAWN HAS NOT YET BROKEN-SWITZ-1973
DAY OF THE IDIOTS-GER-1981
DEAD OF NIGHT-UK-1945
DEADFALL-UK-1968
DEADLY TRAP-FR/IT-1971
DEATH AND FASHION-IT-1989
DEATH OF A BUREAUCRAT-CU-1966
DEATH OF A SOLDIER-AUS-1986
DEATH OF MIKEL-SP-1984
DECEPTIONS-IT-1985
DEEP ILLUSION-UK-1987
DEEP JWELEY JAI-IND-1959
DEVIL IN THE FLESH-FR/IT-1986

DEVIL'S OWN-UK-1966
DIAGNOSIS: MURDER-UK-1974
DOCTOR MABUSE, THE GAMBLER-UK-1922
DOCTORS FROM OH! COPENHAGEN-DEN-1970
DOUBLE BED-FR/IT-1965
DOUBLE NEGATIVE-CAN-1980
DOUBLE SKULLS-AUST-1986
DOWN THE ANCIENT STAIRS-IT/FR-1975
DR. TARR'S TORTURE DUNGEON-MEX-1972
DREAM CASTLE-NOR-1986
DUCK RINGS AT HALF PAST SEVEN-GER/IT-1968
EARTHBOUND-GER-1968
EDITH'S DIARY-GER-1983
ELECTRONIC MONSTER-UK-1958
ENCHANTMENT-JAP-1989
ENDLESS NIGHT-UK-1972
ENJOY! –FR- 1978
EQUUS-UK-1977
EVA...WAS EVERYTHING BUT LEGAL-SWED-1969
EXPLOSION-CAN-1970
FACE OF ANOTHER-JAP-1966
FACE OF DARKNESS-UK-1976
FACE OF TERROR-SP-1962
FACE TO FACE-GER/UK-1969
FACE TO FACE-SWED-1975
FAITHLESS ECKEHART-GER-1931
FANTASM-AUS-1976
FANTASY OF LOVE-GER/FR/IT-1980
FAR AWAY AND CLOSE-SWED-1976
FAREWELL-AUST-1984
FATHER AND SON-GER-1984
FEAR-AUST-1984
FEAR OF FEAR-GER-1975
FEATHERED SHADOWS-CZECH-1930
FEW DAYS WITH ME-FR-1989
FIFTH HORSEMAN IS FEAR-CZECH-1965
FIRE WITHIN-FR/IT-1963
FIRM FOREVER-GER-1984
FIRST NAME: CARMEN-FR-1984
FIVE GOLDEN HOURS-IT/UK-1961
FLIGHT FROM FOLLY-UK-1945
FLYING SAUCERS-MEX-1955
FM~FREQUENCY MURDER-FR-1988
FOLLOW A STAR-UK-1959
FOR THE SAKE OF HEART-IND-1972
FOREVER MY HEART-UK-1954

FORGIVE ME FOR BETRAYING ME-UK-1983
FRANKENSTEIN AND THE MONSTER FROM HELL-UK-1974
FRANKENSTEIN MUST BE DESTROYED-UK-1969
FRENCH EROTIC FANTASIES-FR-1978
FRENZY-UK-1945
FRIEND WILL COME TONIGHT-FR-1946
FRIGHTMARE-UK-1974
FROM THE LIFE OF THE MARIONETTES-GER-1980
FUEGO-ARG-1968
GEHRAYEE-IND-1980
GERMAN SISTERS-GER-1981
GERMANS STRIKE AGAIN-GER-1949
GHOST STORY-UK-1974
GIRL OF THE NIGHT-UK-1960
GLASS TOWER-GER-1957
GODDESSES-UK-1973
GOKE, BODYSNATCHER FROM HELL-JAP-1968
GOODBYE ROBERT-ARG-1985
GOODBYE, SOLIDARITY-NOR-1985
GOTTO GO-GER-1985
GRASS IS SINGING-SWED/UK-1981
GUARDIAN AND HIS POET-GER-1978
GUARDIANS-NOR-1978
GUEST-IT-1984
GUMSHOE-HK-1972
GUY DE MAUPASSANT-FR-1982
HABANERA-CU-1984
HALF OF LOVE-BEL-1985
HALLUCINATIONS IN A DERANGED MIND-UK-1970
HANDS OF THE RIPPER-UK-1975
HANUSSEN-GER/HUN-1988
HAPPY BIRTHDAY TO ME-CAN-1980
HARMLESS LUNATIC'S ESCAPE-UK-1908
HARRER CASE-GER-1986
HEAD AGAINST THE WALLS-FR-1958
HEADSTAND-AUS-1981
HEALTHY MARRIED LIFE-SP-1973
HEAVENS ABOVE-UK-1963
HEINZ IN THE MOON-GER-1934
HELLBOUND: HELLRAISER II-UK-1988
HELTER SKELTER-UK-1949
HENRI-CAN-1986
HENRY IV-IT-1984
HIDDEN ROOM-UK-1948
HIDEOUT-GER-1962
HIMMO, KING OF JERUSALEM-ISR-1987

HOLOCAUST 2000-IT/UK-1977
HONEYBUN; OR, HOW DO I TELL MY DAUGHTER? -GER-1969
HORROR HOSPITAL-UK-1973
HORROR OF DRACULA-UK-1958
HOSPITAL OF THE TRANSFIGURATION-POL-1978
HOSTILE WITNESS-UK-1968
HOT NIGHTS AND DIRTY DAYS-GER-1972
HOURS OF LOVE-IT-1963
HOUSE OF PSYCHOTIC WOMEN-MEX-1974
HOUSE OF THE YELLOW CARPET-IT-1982
HOUSE THAT DRIPPED BLOOD-UK-1971
HOUSE UNDER THE TREES-FR-1971
HOW TO GET AHEAD IN ADVERTISING-UK-1989
HOW TO LOSE A WIFE AND FIND A LOVER-IT-1978
HOW WILLINGLY YOU SING-AUS-1975
HUNCHBACK OF THE MORG-SP-1972
I AM PIERRE RIVIERE-FR-1975
I HATE BLONDES-IT-1981
I LEARNED IT IN PARIS-GER-1960
I LIVE IN FEAR-JAP-1955
I LOVE YOU, I LOVE YOU-FR/SWED-1968
I NEVER CRIED LIKE THIS BEFORE-NETH-1970
I, THE COUNTESS-BUL-1989
ICE AGE-GER/NOR-1975
IDIOTS MAY APPLY-HUN-1986
ILLUMINATION-POL-1972
IMPERATIVE-FR/GER-1982
IMPRECASION-EGY-1984
IMPROPER CHANNELS-CZECH-1981
IN LOVE WITH SEX-FR-1973
IN NEED OF SPECIAL ATTENTION-IT-1981
INKI-GER-1973
INQUISITOR-ARG/PERU-1975
INSIDE AND OUTSIDE-AUS-1983
INSTITUTION-GER-1978
INVISIBLE DR. MABUSE-GER-1962
IT WAS HIM…YES! YES! -IT-1951
JESUS OF MONTREAL-CAN-1989
JOHN THE VIOLENT-GER-1973
JOSHUA THEN AND NOW-CAN-1985
JOURNEY THROUGH THE DREAM-IND-1975
JUDGE-SWED-1960
KAALANGALIL AVAL VASANTHAM-IND-1976
KADUVAYE PIDICHA KIDUVA-IND-1977
KHAMOSHI-IND-1969
KILLER'S MOON-UK-1978

KING IN SHADOW-GER-1957
LABYRINTH-GER-1959
LABYRINTH OF PASSION-SP-1982
LADY ON THE BUS-UK-1978
LAKSHMANA REKHA-IND-1984
LAST ADVENTURE-SWED-1974
LAST JOURNEY-UK-1935
LAST LOVE-GER-1979
LEGAL TRIAL OF CARL-EMMANUEL JUNG-FR-1970
LEGEND OF THE WOLF WOMAN-SP-1977
LESBIAN VAMPIRES-GER/SP-1970
LETHAL FILM-SWED-1988
LIFE IN DANGER-UK-1959
LIFT-NETH-1983
LIGHT FINGERS-UK-1957
LITTLE BUNCH-FR-1983
LITTLE JERK-FR-1984
LIVING DEAD-UK-1932
LONELY HEARTS-AUS-1982
LONG SHOT-UK-1978
LOVES OF KAFKA-ARG-1989
LOW VISIBILITY-CAN-1984
LUDWIG-GER-1972
LUDWIG II-GER-1955
LUNATIC AT LARGE-UK-1921
LUNATICS-FR-1986
MACHINE-FR-1977
MACISTE-IT-1915
MAD HEART-FR-1970
MADE IN BRITAIN-UK-1984
MADELEINE...ANATOMY OF A DREAM-IT-1974
MADHOUSE-UK-1974
MADMAN AT EAR-FR/IT-1985
MADNESS-RUS-1968
MADNESS RULES-SWED-1947
MAGDALENA_POSSESSED BY THE DEVIL-GER-1974
MAGIC CHRISTIAN-UK-1969
MAGIC MOUNTAIN-FR/GER/IT-1982
MAN FACING SOUTHEAST-ARG-1986
MAN FROM THIS STAR-FIN-1958
MAN OF FLOWERS-AUS-1984
MAN ON THE WALL-GER-1982
MAN WHO HAUNTED HIMSELF-UK-1971
MAN WHO KNEW LOVE-SP-1976
MAN WITHOUT A FACE-MEX-1951
MAN WITHOUT MEMORY-GER/SWIT-1984

MANAGEMENT FORGIVES A MOMENT OF MADNESS-VENICE-1979
MANSION OF MADNESS-MEX-1973
MARIA'S HOURS-POR-1979
MARIANA, MARIANA-MEX-1987
MARK-UK-1961
MARTIN'S DAY-CAN-1985
MARY HAD A LITTLE-UK-1961
MARY MY DEAREST-MEX-1982
MASK-CAN-1961
MATADOR-SP-1986
MATCHLESS-AUS-1974
MATRIARCH-IT-1968
MEDUSA TOUCH-FR/UK-1978
MELZER-GER/SWIT-1983
MILLIONAIRESS-UK-1960
MINE OWN EXECUTIONER-UK-1947
MISADVENTURES OF MR. WILT-UK-1989
MIX ME A PERSON-UK-1962
MOI, PIERRE RIVIERE-FR-1975
MONSTER CLUB-UK-1981
MONTENEGRO (PIGS AND PEARLS) –SWED/UK-1981
MORNING AFTER-FR-1909
MOTH-POL-1980
MOTHER'S MEAT AND FREUD'S FLESH-CAN-1984
MR. NICE GUY-CAN-1987
MR. PATMAN-CAN-1980
MURDER BY NIGHT-CAN-1989
MURDER CLINIC-FR/IT-1966
MY DEAREST SENORITA-SP-1971
MY FIRST WIFE-AUS-1984
MY PLEASURE IS MY BUSINESS-CAN-1974
MY WIFE, THE IMPOSTOR-GER-1931
NAKED RUNNER-UK-1967
NANAMI: INFERNO OF FIRST LOVE-JAP-1968
NELLIGAN DOCUMENT-CAN-1969
NEW BLACK EMMANUELLE-IT-1976
NEW LOT-UK-1942
NEXT GENTLEMAN_THE SAME LADY-GER-1968
NIGHT HAIR CHILD-UK-1971
NIGHT WATCH-UK-1973
NIGHTMARE LADY-GER-1981
NINE AGES OF NAKEDNESS-GER-1969
NO PLACE FOR JENNIFER-UK-1949
NOBODY'S WIFE-ARG-1982
NORMAN LOVES ROSE-AUS-1982
NOSFERATU THE VAMPIRE-FR/GER-1979

OLGA AND HER CHILDREN-IT-1985
ONE MONTH LATER-NETH-1987
ORDER-GER-1980
ORDERS TO KILL-UK-1958
ORDINARY MADNESS OF A DAUGHTER OF HAM-FR-1988
ORIGINAL SIN-UK-1948
OTHER-GER-1930
OTHER SIDE OF UNDERNEATH-UK-1972
OTTO_THE NEW MOVIE-GER-1987
OUTRAGEOUS!-CAN-1977
PAGAL-IND-1940
PAGE OF MADNESS-JAP-1926
PAVILION VI-YUG-1979
PEEPING TOM-UK-1960
PERSONA-SWED-1966
PHANTOM OF THE MOULIN ROUGE-FR-1925
PINK PANTHER STRIKES AGAIN-UK-1976
PIZZA TRIANGLE-IT/SP-1970
PLEASURE OF VENGEANCE-MEX-1987
POPE JOAN-UK-1972
POTTERIES-HUN-1981
PRACTICE OF LOVE-GER/AUST-1985
PRICK UP YOUR EARS-UK-1987
PRIVATE POTTER-UK-1962
PRIVATE'S PROGRESS-UK-1956
PROSTITUTION RACKET-IT-1975
PSY-FR-1981
PSYCHO GIRLS-CAN-1984
PSYCHOPATH-IT-1968
PUMPKIN EATER-UK-1964
PUSSY TALK-FR-1975
QUEEN OF THE VAMPIRES-FR-1967
QUESTION OF SILENCE-NETH-1982
QUIET DEATH-GER-1986
QUIET, PLEASE-UK-1938
RANDU PENKUTTIKAL-IND-1978
RAVEN-FR-1943
REBIRTH-IND-1972
REST IS SILENCE-GER-1959
RETURN OF THE PINK PANTHER-UK-1974
RETURN OF THE SOLDIER-UK-1982
REVENGE OF THE PINK PANTHER-UK-1978
RIGHT OF THE MADDEST-FR-1973
ROOM TO LET-UK-1949
ROOM WITH A VIEW OF THE SEA-POL-1978
ROUND MY HEAD IN FORTH DAYS-CAN-1986

RULING CLASS-UK-1972
SAFETY CATCH-FR-1970
SANDHYA MAYANGUM NERAM-IND-1983
SANKHUPUSHPAM-IND-1977
SANTA SANGRE-IT-1989
SCHIZO-UK-1976
SCHOLLER'S INN-GER-1952
SCOTLAND YARD DRAGNET-UK-1957
SCOTLAND YARD HUNTS DR. MABUSE-GER-1963
SCRUBBERS-UK-1982
SECRET CEREMONY-UK-1968
SECRET PLACES-UK-1984
SECRETS OF A SOUL-GER-1926
SECRETS OF A SOUL-GER-1950
SENDER-UK-1982
SEVEN BEAUTIES-IT-1975
SEVEN TIMES A DAY-CAN/US-1971
SEVEN-PER-CENT-SOLUTION-UK-1976
SEVENTH VEIL-UK-1945
SEVERED HEAD-UK-1971
SEX MACHINE-IT-1975
SEXOANALYSIS-ARG-1968
SEXORCIST-IT-1974
SEXTASY-FR-1978
SEXUAL PARTNERSHIP-GER-1968
SHARADA-IND-1973
SHE'S BEEN AWAY-UK-1989
SHINIG ARC-CHI-1989
SHIP WAS LOADED-UK-1957
SHIRLEY THOMPSON VERSUS THE ALIENS-AUS-1968
SHOUT-UK-1978
SI MAMAD-INDO-1973
SILENT PLAYGROUND-UK-1964
SLEEPING TIGER-UK-1954
SLICKERS VS. KILLERS-HK-1989
SMALLER SKY-POL-1981
SOFT ERROR-GER-1982
SOMEBODY'S DARLING-UK-1925
SOMEONE BEHIND THE DOOR-FR/IT-1971
SOMNAMBULISTS-SP-1978
SPACED OUT-UK-1981
SPASMS-CAN-1982
SPIES-FR-1957
SPLIT-UK-1974
SPY-GER-1984
STOP ME BEFORE I KILL-UK-1961

STRAIGHTENING OUT THE BRAIN-FR-1911
SUCCUBUS-GER-1968
SUDDENLY, LAST SUMMER-UK-1959
SURROGATE-CAN-1989
SUSPIRIA-IT-1976
SWAPPERS-UK-1970
SWISSMAKERS-SWIT-1978
TAKE IT EASY MOM-FR-1978
TALES THAT WITNESS MADNESS-UK-1973
TASTE OF EXCITEMENT-UK-1968
TEDDY BAER-SWIT-1983
TEMPEST IN THE FLESH-FR-1954
TEMPTATION-GER-1981
TEMPTER-IT-1978
TEOREMA-IT-1968
TESTAMENT OF DR. MABUSE-GER-1933
THALAVATTAM-IND-1986
THERE GOES THE BRIDE-UK-1980
THEY ARE COMING TO GET YOU-IT/SP-1973
THIN BLUE LINE-ISR-1988
THIRD SECRET-UK-1964
THIRST-AUS-1979
THIS CRAZY WORLD OF OURS-YUG-1970
THIS WAS A WOMAN-UK-1947
THOSE DEAR DEPARTED-AUS-1987
THREE CASES OF MURDER-UK-1955
THREE STRANGE LOVES-SWED-1949
TIE ME UP! TIE ME DOWN!-SP-1989
TO BE SIXTEEN-CAN-1979
TO DIE OF LOVE-FR/IT-1970
TO SEE OR NOT TO SEE-CAN-1972
TONIGHT_EVENTUALLY-GER-1930
TONS OF TROUBLE-UK-1956
TOO PRETTY TO BE HONEST-FR-1972
TOTAL FAMILY-AUST-1981
TRADITIONS, MY ASS-DEN-1979
TULIPS-CAN-1981
TUNNEL-ARG-1952
27 A-AUS-1974
TWICE LIVED-GER-1912
TWO A PENNY-UK-1968
UNDER LOCK AND KEY-GER-1979
UNDER THE DOCTOR-UK-1976
UNFINISHED GAME OF GO-JAP/CHI-1982
UNSPOKEN-IND-1984
US REAL MEN-IT-1987

VANAJA GIRIJA-IND-1975
VENGEANCE OF SHE-UK-1968
VERONIKA VOSS-GER-1982
VICTIM OF PASSION-THAI-1975
VIOLET-YUG-1978
VOICES-POL-1981
VOYAGE TO NOWHERE-SP-1986
WAR OF THE MADMEN-SP-1987
WEDNESDAY'S CHILD-UK-1972
WEEK'S HOLIDAY-FR-1980
WEREWOLF WOMAN-IT-1976
WHAT IN THE WORLD IS GOING ON WITH WILLI?-GER-1970
WHEN THE GODS FALL ASLEEP-UK-1972
WHEREVER YOU ARE-GER/POL/UK-1988
WHISPERERS-UK-1967
WHO'S CRAZY, DOCTOR?-GER-1982
WINKY, PHOTOGRAPHER-UK-1915
WISH YOU WERE HERE-UK-1987
WITHCHCRAFT THROUGH THE AGES-SWED-1920
WITCHES' SABBATH-FR/IT-1988
WITH THE BLOOD OF OTHERS-FR-1974
WOMAN NEXT DOOR-FR-1981
WOMAN WITH RESPONSIBILITIES-GER-1979
WOMEN ARE THAT WAY-UK-1932
WOMEN OF DOOM-SP-1972
WR_MYSTERIES OF THE ORGANISM-YUG-1971
WRONG WORLD-AUS-1985
YOU ARE LYING-SWED-1969
YOUNG FREUD-AUST-1976
YOUR TICKET IS NO LONGER VALID-CAN-1981

Appendix-C

ADDITIONAL INTERNATIONAL MOVIES IN WHICH THE PSYCHIATRISTS ARE DEPICTED
(International Movie Data Base, http://us.imdb.com)

AAGHATA-IND-1994
AATMA BALAM-IND-1964
ABEL-NETH-1986
AIDANKAATAJAR ELI HEIDAN LALKEENSA VEDENPAISUMUS-FIN-1982
ANJALI-IND-1990
ANTEK POLICMAJSTER-POL-1935
ANTWERP KILLER-BEL-1983
ARDILLA ROJA, LA-SP-1993
BILA PANI-CZECH-1965
BOLIVAR SOY YO-COL/FR-2001
BICHO DE SETE CABECAS-BRA-2001
CARRY ON ADMIRAL-UK-1957
CHARLOTTE GRAY-AUS/GER/UK-2001
CHIVARAKU MIGILEDI-IND-1960
CLOCKWORK ORANGE-UK-1971
CTYRI VRAZDY STACI, DRAHOUSKU-CZECH-1970
CUANDO EL MUNDO SE ACABE TE SEGUIRE AMANDO-SP-1998
DEEP JWELEY JAI-IND-1959
DEMONISMENI, I-GRE-1975
DEMONSOUL-UK/US-1994
DER KONIG VON KREUTZBERG-GER-1990
DET BLI'R I FAMILIEN-DEN/SWED-1994
DIARIES OF VASLAV NIJINSKY-AUS/GER/SWED-2001
DIS-MOI QUE JE REVE-FR-1998
DIVKA NA KOSTETI-CZECH-1972
DOBRY VOJAK SVEJK-CZECH-1931
DOLCI SIGNORE, LE-IT-1967
DOMAREN-SWED-1960
DOPPELGANGER-UK-1969
EINE FRAU NAMENS HARRY-GER-1990
EFTYHOS TRELATHIKA-GRE-1961
ELECTROMENAGER-FR-2001
EN ONOMATI TOU NOMOV-GRE-1970
ENRICO IV-IT-1984
ERATOMANE, L'-IT-1974
EUROPA '51-IT-1951
EXTENSION DU DOMAINE DE LA LUTTE-FR-1999
FANY-CZECH-1995
FEI LUNG MAANG JEUNG-HK-1987 [JACKIE CHEN]
4 MOCHE DI VELLUTO GRIGIO-FR/IT-1971
FUTARI-JAP-1991
GOSTI IZ GALAKSIJE-CZECH/YUG-1989

GRAFINYATA, AZ-BUL-1989
HATSUKOI JIGOKUHEN-JAP-1967
HOTEL MODRA HVEZDA-CZECH-1941
HOULIGANS KATO TA HERIA APO TA NIATA-GRE-1983
IKIMONO NO KIROKU-JAP-1955
JA UZ BUDU HODNY, DEDECKU-CZECH-1979
JESTE VETSI BLBEC, REZ JSME DOUFALI-CZECH-1994
KAHDEKSAS VELJES-FIN-1971
KNOFLIKARI-CZECH-1997
KYUA-JAP-1997
KYUKETSUKI GOKEMIDORO-JAP-1968
LEOLO-CAN/FR-1992
LIFT, DE-NETH-1983
MA FEMME EST UNE PANTHERE-FR-1960
MALIZIE DI VENERE, LE-GER/IT/UK-1969
MEINE FREUNDIN SYBELLE-GER-1967
MOTS POUR LE DIRE, LES-FR-1983
MRTVEJ BROUK-CZECH/SLOVAK-1998
MUERTE DE UN BUROCRATA, LA-CU-1966
NAHOTA NA PRODEJ-CZECH-1993
NATIONALE 7-FR-2000
NI LJUGGER-SWED-1969
99.9-SP-1998
N'OBLIE PAS QUE TO VAS MOURIR-FR-1995
NUORIA IHMISIA-FIN-1943
OCCHIOPINOCCHIO-IT/US-1994
ODIO LE BIONDE-FR/GER/IT-1980
ORE DELL'AMORE, LE-IT-1963
OUI, MAIS-FR-2000
PARANO-FR-1980
PETITE AMIE D'ANTONIO, LA-FR-1992
PREA TARZIU-ROM-1996
PRESQUE RIEN-BEL/FR-2000
PROVINCIE, DE-NETH-1991
P'TIT CON-FR-1984
ROMAN DE LULU, LE-FR-2001
RYCHLE POHYBY OCI-CZECH-1998
RYM DINVASION I LAPPLAND-SWED/US-1959
SAPIHES-GER/ISR-1982
SCHUZKA SE STINY-CZECH-1982
SEXE QUI PASLE, LE-FR-1975
7 FOIS...PAR JOUR-CAN/ISR-1971
SHRINK-CAN-1998
SONO OTOKO, KYOBO NI TSUKI-JAP-1989
SRDECNY POZDRAV ZE ZEMEKOULE-CZECH-1982
STORIE DI VITA E MALAVITA-IT-1975

SWAPNADANAM-IND-1976
TANIN NO KAO-JAP-1966
TARANTOLA DAL VENTRE NERO, LA-FR/IT-1972
27A-AUS-1974
UM HOMEM SERIO-BRA-1996
UOMO SENZA MEMORIA, L'-IT-1974
VIE COMMENCE DEMAIN, LE-FR-1949
VRAH SKRYVA TVAR-CZECH-1966
YAMALEELA-IND-1994
YOUR TICKET IS NO LONGER VALID-CAN-1981

Appendix-D

Highlights from the Workshop, "The Good, The Bad and The Ugly", American Psychiatric Association Institute of Psychiatric Services, Orlando, FL, October 10-14, 2001

The Good,

The Bad,

and The Ugly

Hollywood's Portrayal of the Psychiatrists

**Presented
By
Fuat Ulus, M.D. and Eda Ulus, B.S.**

**WORKSHOP 35
1.30 PM – 3.00 PM
Friday, October 12, 2001
APA 53rd Institute, Orlando, FL**

THE THEME OF THE WORKSHOP

FIGHTING STIGMA CENTRALIZED AROUND THE MENTALLY ILL AND MENTAL ILLNESS

Despite our tremendous efforts launched in the recent years, mental illness and the mentally afflicted people continue to be the subject of public ridicule, isolation and apathy. Insurance companies keep limiting the mental health benefits disproportionate to the medical coverage they provide. The society maintains its ignorance hence the fear, the paranoia and the prejudice unfairly as well as unfoundedly generated by the emotionally afflicted fellow human beings.

We seem to be in need of using any tool to educate public, the legislators, the business, the law enforcement officials, the courts and all the other jurisdictions starting in our own community where we live and work. It needs to be something with which all of these fellow citizens from their respective disciplines are familiar for simplicity, practicality and applicability.

What is the element that may have something in common for all of those various people from the different backgrounds?

Yes, ENTERTAINMENT is one of the most popular media vehicles and...

...Yes, WATCHING MOVIES is one of the most effective entertainment variables.

Every judge, football player, police(wo)man, teacher, plumber, construction worker, politician, computer designer, Wall Street wizard, soldier, cleaner and even laid off worker along with all other people from the different trades enjoy movies regardless the gender, ethnical background, race, or age.

Many educators and therapists have already been taking liberty in extending the movies beyond their entertainment purposes into the education and treatment during the last decades. The presenters of this workshop therefore, have designed the material to provide the participants information as well as experience enabling them to spread the word in the locations where they practice and use the movies different from The One Flew over the Cuckoo's Nest or The Silence of the Lambs!

It has been unfortunate that the movie industry of Hollywood has always been capitalizing on the sensationalism, fiction and/or unrealistic scenarios for the obvious financial return expectations. However, unlike the public belief, we know so many Hollywood films in which the passionate, compassionate, competent and/or caring clinicians are portrayed.

Do you know, for example, that there have been more than 1200 US productions in which the psychiatrists are depicted between 1906 and 2002?

That means that Hollywood came out with the movie with a psychiatrist portrayal; averaging one in every 25 some days for 96 years!

Again, do you know that "The Good" psychiatrist portrayals constitute more than 60% of those films?

That again means that there are competent and caring silver screen colleagues presented in more than 750 productions!

This is a tremendous material and infinite educational potential that nobody can ignore... not even Hollywood!

We need to get in touch with the public and community organizations of our regional practice regions to show these films and/or their important clips in scheduled times and places.

Remember, the human beings never forget the experience they have under two opposite settings: Painful times and pleasurable moments. Of course, we leave the pain out of this process. The only other option we have is pleasure. Entertain the public and the officials while educating them is something they do not forget.

So, what are we waiting for?

Let us have fun-filled and exciting 90 minutes to watch, observe, laugh, cry, discuss and exchange ideas about this mission. One of the old sayings reminds us that the travel necessitating months to complete starts with taking the first step. Well, welcome taking our first step in this workshop!

"THE GOOD" MOVIE PSYCHIATRISTS

These clinicians are competent, empathic, compassionate and/or passionate in approaching the patient; provide everything for their well being while adequately and appropriately honor the professional boundaries set forth by the contemporary ethics. We see them in the dramas most of the time.

"THE BAD" MOVIE PSYCHIATRISTS

The psychiatrists who receive the patients within the jurisdiction of their work but either intentionally or inadvertently end up harming them through omission, e.g. incompetence, or commission, e.g. using the patients for their financial, social, or sociopathic personal purposes. The comedies usually depict them.

"THE UGLY" MOVIE PSYCHIATRIST

Here we have those shrinks whose relationships with the patients are within the line of psychopathy violating clinical, ethical, spiritual and legal boundaries altogether.

...AND THE OTHERS

Sergio Leone's "Spaghetti Westerns" bring us quite a realistic dimension of the West we have not seen in Tom Mix, Charles Starrett, "Wild" Bill Elliott, Tex Ritter and Roy Rogers flicks. Even Gary Cooper, John Wayne and Randolph Scott era is quite clear regarding the differentiation of good people with white hats versus bad people with black hats. One cannot clarify easily, however, the difference between The Good ANTIHERO and the Bad & the Ugly EVIL ONES in those Spaghetti Westerns.

The same may be applicable to the screen psychiatrists hence the title of this workshop!

It is difficult to perceive the silver screen clinician at times for many reasons:

1) There are very few movies scenarios of which are based solely on the psychiatrist character in the picture. The audience may or may not find adequate space & time to review the clinician's conduct.
2) The most depictions describe "supportive actor & actress" roles with not much substance.
3) The rest are nothing but "glimpse" portrayals for the better or worse.
4) "The woods versus the trees" phenomenon confuses the perception. A clinician who may be "The Good" psychiatrist for that given moment in the movie may actually be "The Bad" within the entirety of the film.
5) The general audience may celebrate "The Good" shrink for his/her falling in love with the patient hence addressing the romance of the picture while the real life colleagues curse him/her for being "The Bad" regarding the violation of professional boundaries.
6) The psychiatrists' ethnical and socio-cultural value system may have an impact on this "classification." The clinician with the background of properly hugging the patients may have quite difficult time adapting the strictly enforced ethical principles set forth by the region's authorities.

Bottom line?

Select "The Good" movies in which the psychiatrists are well characterized and ready to explain the realistic as well as unrealistic features to educate the public and community agencies along with organizations.

THE SPECIAL NOTE FOR THE LADY PSYCHIATRISTS PORTRAYED IN HOLLYWOOD PRODUCTIONS

The portrayal of the psychiatrist in the Hollywood movies has always been reflective of the political and socio-familial movements, changes and value systems throughout the decades. The depiction of the female psychiatrists, however, has not been affected by these variables.

Regardless the production year of given motion picture, the lady psychiatrists in the US movies have always been single, unhappily married, abused, separated and/or divorced. Their approaches to the patients are based more on the typical female traditions such as maternal instincts and nurturing qualities rather than those professional and ethical principles. They almost always fall in love with the leading male characters portrayed as the patients in the films! They are either "cured" by their male patients or become the love objects of the said characters at the end of the most movies. I personally do not remember many movies in which a leading, happily married, mother of two, competent lady behavioral clinician helping her male-or female-patient without falling in love!

One of the rare portrayals, perhaps the one comes closest to the said achievement, was the movie, "Wild in the Country (1961)" in which the lady psychiatrist (Hope Lange) almost falls in love with her patient (Elvis Presley) but keeps the professional boundaries relatively intact and returns back to her practice following the successful treatment of the young man.

Hollywood has been very reluctant to accept the fact that the lady clinicians may be as "Good" in their professional competence and conduct as handling their personal and familial affairs.

Hollywood Psychiatrists Trivia

THE SAMPLES OF "THE GOOD PSYCHIATRIST" MOVIES

As Good as It Gets (1997), Bell Jar (1979), Captain Newman, MD (1964), Caretakers (1963), Crazy People (1990), Don Juan de Marco (1995), Don't Say a Word (2002), Dream Team (1989), Fear Strikes Out (1957), Fine Madness (1966), High Wall (1947), I Never Promised You the Rose Garden (1977), Instinct (1999), Kid (2000), Now, Voyager (1942), Ordinary People (1980), Snake Pit (1948), Terminal Man (1974), Three Faces of Eve (1957), 12 Monkeys (1995), Who's Life is It Anyway?" (1981)

THE SAMPLES OF "THE BAD PSYCHIATRIST" MOVIES

Airplane II (1983), Awakenings (1990), Backdraft (1991), Blue Sky (1994), Caine Mutiny (1954), Crazy People (1990), Deer Hunter (1978), Don't Say a Word (2002), Dr. Doolittle (1998), Final Analysis (1992), Fine Madness (1966), Locket (1946), Mr. Frost (1990), Nuts (1987), One Flew Over the Cuckoo's Nest (1975), Second Serve (1986), Snake Pit (1948), Some Kind of Hero (1982), Take the Money and Run (1969), Something About Mary (1998), What About Bob? (1991), What's New Pussycat? (1965), Who's Life is It, Anyway? (1981)

THE SAMPLES OF "THE UGLY PSYCHIATRIST" MOVIES

American Perfekt (1997), Conspiracy Theory (1997), Disturbed (1990), Dr. Giggles (1992), Dressed to Kill (1980), Fine Madness (1966), Halloween (1978), Halloween 2 (1981), Halloween 4 (1988), Halloween 5 (1989), Hannibal (2001), High Anxiety (1977), House of Cards (1968), Manhunter (1986), Nightbreed (1990), Shock (1946), Silence of the Lambs (1991), Surviving the Game (1994)

THE FIRST MOVIE PORTRAYAL OF THE PSYCHIATRIST

Dr. Dippy's Sanitarium (1906)

THE FIRST MOVIE BASED ON ACTUAL CASE HISTORY OF A PATIENT WRITTEN BY A PSYCHIATRIST [DR. MORTON PRINCE, THE DISSOCIATION OF PERSONALITY, THE CASE OF SALLY BEAUCHAMP, 1905]

The Case of Becky (1915), The Case of Becky (1921)

THE PERFORMER APPEARING AS THE SAME PSYCHIATRIST IN THE ORIGINAL MOVIE AND THE SEQUELS

Donald Pleasance

Halloween (1978), Halloween 2 (1981), Halloween 4 (1988), Halloween 5 (1989)

Mary Ellen Trainor

Lethal Weapon (1987), Lethal Weapon 2 (1989), Lethal Weapon 3 (1992), Lethal Weapon 4 (1998)

THE PSYCHIATRISTS ARGUING ABOUT THE QUALITY CARE

Crazy People (1990), Dream Team (1989), Fine Madness (1966), High Anxiety (1977), Nightmare on the Elm Street 5 (1989), Silent Madness (1984)

THE FIRST AFRICAN-AMERICAN ARMY PSYCHIATRIST

Manchurian Candidate (1968)

THE FIRST UNCENSORED X-RATED MOVIE

[PSYCHIATRIST PORTRAYAL!]

The Immoral Mr. Teas (1959)

THE MOVIE, PORTRAYING PSYCHIATRISTS, THAT WAS ALLEGEDLY REVIEWED BY THE US SENATE PRIOR TO THE MH/MR MENTAL HEALTH ACT OF 1963

Caretakers (1963)

THE HIGHES NUMBER OF THE PSYCHIATRISTS PORTRAYED IN ONE MOVIE

[FIVE!]

Fine Madness (1966)

PSYCHIATRIST TURNS TERRORIST

House of Cards (1968)

PSYCHIATRIST TURNS COMMUNIST SPY

Big Jim McLain (1952)

PSYCHIATRIST TURNS NAZI SPY

Dangerously They Live (1942)

PSYCHIATRIST TURNS DEDECTIVE

Still of the Night (1982)

PSYCHIATRISTS IN THE COURT

Airplane II (1983), Anatomy of a Murder (1959), Caine Mutiny (1954), Final
Analysis (1992), Nuts (1987), Who's Life is It, Anyway? (1981)

THE LONGEST TITLE OF THE MOVIE SHRINK

[SCOTT ELLIOTT, MD, PHD, MS, PSYCHOLOGIST!]

The Dark Mirror (1946)

THE FIRST SCI-FI FLICK WITH PSYCHIATRIST PORTRAYAL HOWEVER
VERY SHORT

Them (1954)

THE FIRST FILM REVIEWED BY THE WELL KNOWN AND REPUTABLE
MENTAL HEALTH PROFESSIONAL

[OTTO FENICHEL, THE PSYCHOANALYTIC THEORY OF NEUROSIS, 1945]

Lady in the Dark (1944)

BIOPICS & BIOGRAPHIES OF THE POPULAR PSYCHIATRISTS

Freud (1964), Independence [Dr. Benjamin Rush] (1976), Stairway to Light [Dr. Philippe Pinel] (1945)

PSYCHIATRIST IMPERSONATIONS IN THE MOVIES

Bedtime Story (1964), Couch in New York (1996), Couch Trip (1988), Hollow Triumph (1948)

THE FIRST FEMALE ARMY PSYCHIATRIST

Sad Sack (1957)

THE FIRST CHILD PSYCHIATRY MOVIE

[PLAY THERAPY]

Shadow on the Wall (1950)

THE MOVIES WITH CHILD & ADOLESCENT PSYCHIATRY THEMES

Bell Jar (1979), Good Will Hunting (1998), House of Cards (1992), I Never Promised You a Rose Garden (1977), Ordinary People (1980), Splendor in the Grass (1961)

VAMC PSYCHIATRIST PORTRAYALS

Teresa (1951), Article 99 (1998)

THE REAL LIFE PSYCHIATRISTS PORTRAYING THE SCREEN CLINICIANS

[DONALD MUHICH, MD]

Down and Out in Beverly Hills (1986), Bob, Carol, Ted and Alice (1969), Blume in Love (1973)

[DEAN R. BROOKS, MD]

One Flew over the Cuckoo's Nest (1975)

PSYCHIATRIST HAVING A SESSION WITH EMOTIONALLY AFFLICTED
INTERNAL MEDICINE COLLEAGUE

Hospital (1971)

PSYCHIATRIST AS A GROUP THERAPY PATIENT

See You in the Morning (1989)

PSYCHIATRIST TREATING THE TRANSEXUAL OPHTHALMOLOGIST
COLLEAGUE

Second Serve (1986)

THE PERFORMER WHO PORTRAYS THE HIGHEST NUMBER OF THE
PSYCHIATRISTS IN THE MOVIES

[DAVID BISSELL-FIVE TIMES!]

Caine Mutiny (1954), Invasion of the Body Snatchers (1956), I was a Teenage
Werewolf (1957), Third of a Man (1962), Once You Kiss a Stranger (1969)

GANGSTER TURNS PSYCHIATRIST

CRIME DOCTOR movies produced between 1943 and 1949

THE FIRST PSYCHIATRIST MOVIE WITH AA PRESENTATION

Come Fill the Cup (1951)

THE MOVIE IN WHICH THE WORD "PSYCHOANALYST" WAS USED FOR
THE FIRST TIME

Boomerang (1925)

THE FIRST MOVIE IN THAT THE THEME OF HOMOSEXUALITY WAS
SCREENPLAYED

Children of Loneliness (1937)
FRED ASTAIRE AS A PSYCHIATRIST?

[YOU BET!}

Carefree (1938)

THE FIRST HORROR MOVIE IN TECHNICOLOR

[PSYCHIATRIST PORTRAYAL!]

Doctor X (1932)

SAME SCRIPT WITH DIFFERENT REMAKES IN THAT THE SAME
PSYCHIATRIST CHARACTER IS PORTRAYED

Front Page (1931), His Girl Friday (1940), Front Page (1974)

PSYCHIATRIST IN THE WESTERN?

[YEP, YOU RECKON, PARTNER!]

Bronco Billy (1980)

HAS ANY PERFORMER EVER PLAYED THE GOOD, THE BAD AND THE
UGLY IN DIFFERENT MOVIES?

[ROBERT CUMMINGS DID!]

Kings Row [The Good] (1942), What a Way to Go [The Bad] (1964), Promise Her
Anything [The Ugly] (1966)

THE ACTORS AND ACTRESSES WHO HAVE BEEN ON THE BOTH SIDES OF THE PSYCHIATRIC COACH-BY ALPHABETICAL ORDER

EDDIE ALBERT
Psychiatrist *(The Teahouse of the August Moon-1956)*
Patient *(Captain Newman, MD-1964)*

ALAN ARKIN
Psychiatrist *(Gross Pointe Blank-1997)*
Patient *(full Moon High-1981)*

RICHARD DREYFUSS
Psychiatrist *(What About Bob?-1991)*
Patient *(Whose Life Is It Anyway-1981)*

JANE FONDA
Psychiatrist *(Agnes of God-1985)*
Patient *(Klute-1971)*

RICHARD GERE
Psychiatrist *(The Final Analysis-1992)*
Patient *(Mr. Jones-1993)*

ANTHONY HOPKINS
Psychiatrist *(Silence of the Lambs-1991)*
Patient *(Instinct-1999)*

TOMMY LEE JONES
Psychiatrist *(The House of Cards-1992)*
Patient *(Blue Sky-1994)*

GREGORY PECK
Psychiatrist *(Captain Newman, MD-1964)*
Patient *(Mirage-1965)*

BARBRA STREISAND
Psychiatrist *(The Prince of Tides-1991)*
Patient *(Nuts-1987)*

JOANNE WOODWARD
Psychiatrist *(They Might Be Giants-1971)*
Patient *(Three Faces of Eve-1957)*

Appendix-E

The list of the Author's presentations related to the commercial movies and their use in the education & therapy

GROUP MOVIE THERAPY PRESENTATIONS CHAIRED, CO-CHAIRED AND PRESENTED BY THE AUTHOR

Workshop, "The Good, the Bad and the Ugly, Hollywood's Portrayal of the Psychiatrists", American Psychiatric Association, Institute of Psychiatric Services, Annual Meeting, Orlando, FL, October 2001

Second presenter following the primary speaker during Eli & Lilly dinner presentation in Erie, PA, January 2002 (No financial arrangements or obligations with Eli & Lilly)

Workshop, "Group Movie Therapy", Stairways Outpatient Clinic, Erie, PA, January 2002

Workshop, "Group Movie Therapy", Community Integration, Inc. Outpatient Clinic, Erie, PA, February 2002

Second presenter following the primary speaker during Eli & Lilly dinner presentation in Pittsburgh, PA, March 2002 (No financial arrangements or obligations with Eli & Lilly)

Workshop, "The Group Therapy through the Film Clips", University of Pitt, Pittsburgh, PA, April 2002

Primary speaker during Glaxo dinner presentation in Erie, PA, May 2002 (No financial arrangements or obligations with Glaxo)

Workshop, "Motion Pictures, the Therapeutic Modality of the 21st Century", American Psychiatric Association, Annual Meeting, Philadelphia, PA, May 2002

Poster, "Movie Clips, the Powerful Tools of Mental Health Education on Stigma", American Psychiatric Association, Institute of Psychiatric Services, Chicago, IL, October 2002

Conference, "Movie Clips, the Powerful Tools of Mental Health Education on Stigma", NAMIECO, Mercyhurst College, Erie, PA, January 2003

Conference, "Group Movie Therapy", Business Women Roundtable, Erie, PA, January 2003

Workshop, "Group Movie Therapy", International Group Therapy Association, Annual Conference, Istanbul, Turkey, August 2003

Appendix-F

THE MOVIES, EDUCATION, TREATMENT AND HEALING NETWORK!

It has been amazing to find out that many psychiatrists, psychologists, social workers, instructors, and educators have been using movies in their educational and therapeutic settings for decades. Yet, these practitioners have not necessarily been in touch with each other relevant to their work.

The author realizing these successful but sporadic practices started to form, maintain and promote a voluntary e-mail group, members consisting either of providers with expertise in the area or those mental health care providers who would be interested in such a modality.

At the time of this writing, the group has thirty professionals including two members from Canada, one from the United Kingdom and one from Finland. We share our experiences, expertise, inquiries and fun on this listserv. Those with websites display the information relevant to the products of the other members such as websites, books, articles, seminars, etc.

You are quite welcome to join us if such a group is of interest to you.

Visit www.movietx.yourmd.com and/or write uluslar4@aol.com

REFERENCES

Presently, it is very difficult to list or classify all websites, articles, books and all other information about movie/cinema/film/reel therapy in general and group movie therapy in particular not to mention that any list would be outdated within a short time due to constant and continuous developments in the educational, therapeutic and movie industry settings.

The educators and/or therapists using this modality have different studies documented in various jurisdictions, making the classification even more difficult due to the said heterogeneity. Therefore, the following list extracted mainly from the cyberspace and communications among the mental health care providers offers some tips and leads the reader who would like to seek further information about the subject.

There are many books, articles and websites studying the relationship between the psychiatry and movies, but unless presented specifically in some parts of the given publications and presentations, they do not necessarily provide information relevant to the movies and their role in educational as well as therapeutic settings. Therefore, they are not necessarily included in the following list.

Those websites presenting the lists of those movies stories of which address the specific themes, e.g. anxiety, relationship, problem solving, PTSD, co-dependence, depression and etc are included for the readers who like to use them and/or their clips in their educational and/or therapeutic settings.

Kindly keep in mind that the more practitioners and educators the longer the list in the future.

BOOKS

Professor Dr. Gary Solomon, a.k.a. The Movie Doctor from Henderson, Nevada authored two books, "*The Motion Picture Prescription: Watch This Movie, and Call Me in the Morning. 200 Movies to Help You Heal Life's Problems*" and "*Reel Therapy.*" He informed his colleagues in The Movies, Education, Treatment and Healing Network that his third book relevant to children and adolescents has been ready for publication.

"Rent Two Films and Let's Talk in the Morning: Using Popular Movies in Psychotherapy", second edition has been published by John W. Hesley and Jan G. Hesley.

Nancy K. Peske and Beverly West first brought us, *"Cinematherapy: The Girl's Guide to Movies for Every Mood"* and its sequel, *"Advanced Cinematherapy: The Girl's Guide to Finding Happiness."*

Sharon Packer, MD is the author of *"Dreams in Myth, Medicine and Movies."* Her website is listed in the next section.

WEBSITES

Conni Sharp, EdD, Associate Professor, Pittsburg State University, Kansas has one of the pioneering sites at
http://members.tripod.com/cinematherapy/discussion2.html
She has been the co-chair of my workshop, *"Motion Pictures: Therapeutic Modality of the 21st Century"* presented during the American Psychiatric Association's Annual Meeting held in Philadelphia, PA between May 18-23, 2002.

University of Chicago has quite an exclusive site at
http://psychclerk.bsd.uchicago.edu/movies.html
where one may get a mixture of books, articles and further web sites.

The Social Work Department of Middle Tennessee State University offers a course *"God's Hollywood: Movies about Spirituality"* at
http://www.mtsu.edu/~socwork/frost/god/index.html
They provide a couple of phrases verbalized in the vignettes, which may be very useful for group movie therapy.

http://www.azcentral.com/rep/style/articles/cinematherapy27.html site provides the article, *"Pick the Movie to Move Your Mood and It's More Than Entertainment-It's Cinematherapy"* by Gary Soulsman, *the Wilmington News Journal*, March 26, 2001.

Check the site,
http://www.ohio.com/bj/fun/movie/reviews/012000/003987.htm
if you are interested reading, *"Films are Medicine in Cinematherapy"* by
Stephanie Allmon.

Do not miss Daniel Mangin's cinematherapy article published in *the Reader's
Guide to Contemporary Authors,*
http://www.salon.com/health/feature/1999/05/27/film_therapy/index1.html

Chicago Institute for the Moving Image (CIMI) has interesting programs including
cinema therapy at
http://www.cimi.ws/three/kinth.shtml

The Sacramento Bee's Movie Club,
http://www.movieclub.com/news/analyze/analyze.html
presents Alison Roberts' article, *"Analyze This: Psychocinema Offers Movie
Watchers-and Patients-Entertainment and a Dose of Therapy"*, published on
March 22, 2000.

The same author has another article, *"Latest Form of Therapy: Go Rent a Movie"*
published on April 12, 2000 at
http://www.detnews.com/2000/features/0004/12/e06-35051.htm

Clever Magazine's "Movie Therapy 101" by Christopher J. Stephens is at
http://www.clevermag.com/movies/essays/2001movies.htm

Dr. Pam Martin is the author of *Make It Reel, Introduction to Movie Therapy* in
Region 5 Behavioral Health Resources at
http://www.region5rcc.org/Movies/reel%20index%202.htm
She presents worksheets for the group movie therapists through the
exemplification of six popular movies.

http://www.filmtx.com provides very interesting film therapy topics.
Patti Nolan, LCSW, BCD coordinates seminars relevant to the subject.

Fantasy Men Island site has an interesting article, *"Cinema Therapy: Better Living Through Celluloid'"* at
http://aolhometown.planetout.com/romance/fmi/news/article.html?sernum=476

Review the cinema group therapy schedules of Prestera Center at
http://www.prestera.org/support_and_therapy_groups_offer.htm

Study the works of Florida Institute of Technology on Psycho Cinema at
http://www.fit.edu/caps/cinema.html

John W. Hesley provides very credible evolution of cinematherapy from the bibliotherapy in his article, *"Using Popular Movies in Psychotherapy"* published in *Healthy Me/In the News* transcribed from USA Today, January 1, 2001 at
http://www.ahealthyme.com/article/iac/100547975

http://www.lovetips.com/cinematherapy.html presents information about the subject.

"Searching for Inner Meg" is the article of Hank Stuever from *LA WEEKLY,* which can be reviewed at
http://www.laweekly.com/ink/01/23/wls-stuever.shtml

Bernie Wooder, UKCP, MISSM, a movie therapist from the United Kingdom shares his expertise at
http://www.themovietherapist.com

Pekka Lehto, psychiatric nurse and movie therapist from Finland shares his exciting work at
http://koti.mbnet.fi/plehto/movie.html

Sharon Packer, MD whose book is listed in the previous section also has a website at ***http://www.sharon_packer_md.yourmd.com***

http://www.fit.edu/caps/cinema.html provides the list of some movies proportionate to the educational and treatment themes.

Susan Nicosia, Associate Professor, Social Sciences and Humanities, Daniel Webster College gives quite a long list of references presented in *Psychology, Psychiatry and the Movies* and links the site to *Filmography: Movies and Mental Illness* at
http://faculty.dwc.edu/nicosia/moviesandmentalillnessbibliography.htm

Ruth Levine, MD, University of Texas Medical Branch has another useful list of those movies effective in educational and therapeutic settings at
http://www.dartmouth.edu/~admsep/resources.html

Alison Kerr's article, *"Depression can be put in the picture"* about using 'movie therapy' to treat people suffering emotional problems and its gaining increasing acclamation in the US can be reviewed at
http://www.theherald.co.uk/films/archieve/16-8-19101-20-48-16.html

A very comprehensive website reflective of cinema therapy is presented by Birgit Wolz, Ph.D., MFT at ***http://www.cinematherapy.com***

One can find almost everything about what s/he is looking for relevant to the subject.

Last but not least, Fuat Ulus, MD presents information relevant to Group Movie Therapy and provides multiple links on his website at *http://www.movietx.yourmd.com*

ARTICLES

"The Life Stories of Children and Adolescents, Using Commercial Films as Teaching Aids"; *Academic Psychiatry*, 24:4, Winter 2000 and *"The Media: Relationships to Psychiatry and Children"*; *Academic Psychiatry, 26:3,* Fall 2002, by Adrian Sondheimer, MD including references and guidance of the given movies may be asked by writing to Dr. Sondheimer at ***sondhean@umdnj.edu***

"Cinematherapy: Theory and Application"; by Berg-Cross L, Jennings P, Baruch R, Psychotherapy in Private Practice 1990; 8:135-156.

The School of Education, The University of Alabama at Birmingham has an excellent list of valid and reliable research papers at ***http://www.ed.uab.edu/cinematherapy/readings***.

Conni Sharp whose website has listed previously published *Cinematherapy: Metaphorically Promoting Therapeutic Change"*, *Counseling Psychology Quarterly, 2002* and would be reached at ***csharp@pittstate.edu*** if anybody would be interested in getting the copy of article.

We will expect the Internet to be the source of this ever progressing educational and treatment modality in the near future. The reader's regular use of search engines to extract information about this exciting educational and therapeutic tool will be helpful to gather refined information in years to come.

ABOUT THE AUTHOR

EDUCATION

Istanbul University, Faculty of Medicine, Turkish Republic
1968

PROFESSIONAL EXPERIENCE

Full time psychiatrist, Presque Isle Psychiatric Associates, Inc., Erie, PA, Milcreek Community Hospital, Behavioral Health Unit in affiliation with Lake Erie College of Osteopathic Medicine (LECOM), Erie, PA, Stairways Behavioral Health Outpatient Clinic, Erie, PA, teaching college students rotating on inpatient and outpatient settings, inpatient and outpatient psychiatric evaluations, consultation& liaison, med-checks and related services
July 2002-Present

Full time psychiatrist, Presque Isle Psychiatric Associates, Inc., Erie, PA, Community Integration, Inc. (CII), Erie, PA, outpatient psychiatric evaluations, med-checks and related services
November 2001-June 2002

Team Psychiatrist, Assertive Community Treatment Programs, SE PA area, Northampton & Lehigh Counties, Allentown-Bethlehem-Easton axis, crisis residential unit coverage, partial hospitalization program, dual-diagnosis program, visiting & follow up with the patients in the community
August 1998-October 2001

Staff Psychiatrist, St. Luke's Hospital, Bethlehem, PA, General Hospital inpatient, partial and outpatient services, teaching, D&A and C&L services
January 1996-August 1998

Staff Psychiatrist, Altoona Hospital, Altoona, PA, General Hospital inpatient, partial and outpatient services, teaching, Geriatric Assessment Program, D&A and C&L services, Van Zandt VAMC part-time assignment, court evaluations, private practice
June 1984-December 1995   (OVER)

Staff Psychiatrist, Harrisburg Institute of Psychiatry, Harrisburg Hospital, Harrisburg, PA, General Hospital inpatient, partial and outpatient services, teaching, C&L services
July 1983-May 1984

Assistant Professor, University of South Dakota, Medical School, Department of Psychiatry, Sioux Falls, SD, inpatient and outpatient services, teaching, C&L services, Behavioral Medicine Liaison Officer of the Family Medicine Residency Training Program, VAMC services
November 1978-June 1983

Staff Psychiatrist, Warren State Hospital, North Warren, PA, Geriatric Building
November 1974-November 1978

Psychiatric Resident Physician, Warren State Hospital, North Warren, PA
October 1971-November 1974

Medical Director, Boehringer Sohn, Ingelheim am Rhein, Istanbul, Turkey
October 1970-October 1971

Medical Military Officer (Mandatory Military Service), Turkish Armed Forces, Uzunkopru, Turkey
May 1969-October 1970

Sales Representative, Boehringer Sohn, Ingelheim am Rhein, Istanbul, Turkey
October 1968-April 1969

CREDENTIALS

ECFMG, Istanbul, Turkey, February 1969

Board Certification in Psychiatry and Neurology, New Orleans, Louisiana 1979

AMA & APA Continuous Medical Education Certificate, valid through
September 2003

Licensed to practice Medicine & Surgery in PA and NY   (OVER)

ASSOCIATION MEMBERSHIPS

American & Pennsylvania Medical Association
Erie County Medical Society (District Branch)
American & Pennsylvania Psychiatric Association
Western Pennsylvania Psychiatric Society (District Branch)
American Association of Community Psychiatrists
American Association of Emergency Psychiatrists
Association of Organizational & Occupational Psychiatry
International Transactional Analysis Association (ITAA)

PRESENTATIONS

Lehigh Valley Assertive Community Treatment Program, poster presentation, American Psychiatric Association Institute of Psychiatric Services, annual meeting, Philadelphia, PA, October 2000

The Good, The Bad and The Ugly, Hollywood's Portrayal of the Psychiatrists, workshop presentation, co-chaired by Eda Ulus, BS, first year student of Texas Tech, PhD Graduate Program, Counseling Psychology, Lubbock, Texas, American Psychiatric Association, Institute of Psychiatric Services, annual meeting, Orlando, FL, October 2001

Psychiatrist Seeks Healing through Film Clips, Erie Times-News interview, Movie Group Therapy, March 24, 2002

Analyze This! Film clips in the Group Therapy, conference, University of Pittsburgh, Pittsburgh, PA, April 2002

Motion Pictures: The Therapeutic Modality of the 21st Century, workshop presentation, co-chaired by Eda Ulus, BS and Conni Sharp, EdD, Associate Professor, University of Pittsburg, Kansas, American Psychiatric Association, annual meeting, Philadelphia, PA, May 2002

Local ABC TV interview, Focus on Erie, Movie Group Therapy, broadcasted on June 16, 2002

Movie Clips: The Powerful Tools of Community Mental Health Education on Stigma, poster presentation & discussion, American Psychiatric Association, Institute of Psychiatric Services, annual meeting, Chicago, IL, October 2002

(OVER)

(IV)

The author has been married to Fusun from his native Turkish Republic. They have been the lucky parents of two daughters; Eda, a second year Counseling Psychology PhD Program of Texas Tech, Lubbock, Texas and Ece, a graduate of the University of Pittsburgh, Pittsburgh, PA on German and Political Sciences, seeking MA degree in teaching relevant to Teaching English as a Second Language in overseas.